Perspectives on African Governance

fredskorpset
utveksling for utvikling

© IDASA 2006

ISBN 1-920118-14-4 ISBN - 13: 978-1-920118-14-3

Published by the Institute for Democracy in South Africa (IDASA)
6 Spin St
Cape Town, South Africa
8001

Website: www.idasa.org

Produced by IDASA Publishing Department
Editing and design: Page Arts
Cover design: Magenta Media

Perspectives on African Governance

Edited by

Lindlyn Chiwandamira

and

Monica Makaula

Table of contents

Preface

Fredskorpset

Fredskorpset enables young people from different parts of the world to meet and work together. We believe that such meetings result in people learning from one another, enriching their experience. This knowledge is important to those travelling abroad, to the hosts and to the employers.

Fredskorpset believes "partnership for development" is the way to strengthen understanding between North and South in a globalised world and to increase expertise in international questions. Fredskorpset is therefore calling on Norwegian companies, enterprises and organisations to enter into partnerships with enterprises in the South with a view to exchanging personnel and expertise. Such an exchange can attract financial support from Fredskorpset.

Those who travel abroad as Fredskorpset participants are aged between 22 and 35 and work for the partners for a period of one to three years. Exchanges are both ways; North to South and South to North. Fredskorpset no longer sends out participants itself, but calls upon companies and organisations to do so. It is the partner that decides what expertise the person travelling abroad needs to do the job agreed on.

A brief history of the Norwegian Fredskorpset

Fredskorpset (Volunteer Service) was formed on 4 April 1963. It was a product of the political currents of the time – pacifism, non-violence, humanism and Christian traditions – and emerged out of proposals for a peace corps mooted by Norwegian youth organisations. At the time young people saw a peace corps as an expression of solidarity with the world poor, with the focus on developing countries and their needs. Norwegian Development Aid (which later became NORAD) had just been formed, in 1962, and the Norwegian Peace Corps (see Storting Report No. 23 (1961-62)) was created as a sub-division of NORAD. More than 1 500 Norwegians served in the original Peace Corps from 1963 to 2000.

To meet the needs of the partner countries the Norwegian Peace Corps recruited agronomists, health workers and teachers. The Peace Corps had three goals:

- To contribute to the economic and technical progress of developing countries;
- To promote human contact and understanding across national boundaries;
- To allow idealistic and motivated young people to work for what they believe in.

The new Fredskorpset – background

In Storting Proposition No. 1 (1998-99) the government concluded that the Peace Corps in its present form had outlived its usefulness and in Storting Proposition No. 67 (1998-99) presented the overarching goals and principles for restructuring the Peace Corps. As part of its consideration of the "Development Policy Report from the Minister for Development and Human Rights", (see Storting Recommendation No. 28 (1999-2000)) on 18 November 1999 the Storting gave its approval to the government's restructuring of the Peace Corps. In the light of this on 10 December 1999 the Storting passed the appropriations for Fredskorpset for 2000, in accordance with Storting Budgetary Recommendation No. 3 (1999-2000) of 3 December 1999.

Objectives

Fredskorpset aims to help implement the overarching objectives of Norway's co-operation with developing countries: to contribute to permanent improvements in economic, social and political conditions for the people of developing countries, with special emphasis on aid benefiting the poorest of the poor. To this end,

Fredskorpset aims particularly to realise the objective of a more just world order based on fundamental human rights. With this in mind, Fredskorpset will contribute to the creation of contact and co-operation between individuals, organisations and institutions in Norway and in the developing countries, based on solidarity, equality and reciprocity. Fredskorpset will direct its funding to measures aimed at countries that are classified by the Organisation for Economic Co-operation and Development (OECD) as potential recipients of Official Development Assistance (ODA). Of this, at least half will go to the Least Developed Countries (LDCs).

Tasks

Among its objectives are the following:

- To promote reciprocal learning;
- To help participants integrate their know-how and experience into their own societies;
- To help develop and strengthen civil society in developing countries;
- To strengthen local organisations and democratic structures in developing countries;
- To enhance citizens' ability to set and achieve their own development goals;
- To promote greater participation by developing countries in international co-operation.

To achieve these objectives, Fredskorpset will organise the recruitment and training of participants as well as various forms of collaboration:

- Between Norwegian organisations and institutions and those in the developing countries, as well as between organisations and institutions in the developing countries which have established co-operation with Norwegian organisations and institutions (South-South co-operation);
- In Norway, between Norwegian organisations and institutions and those in the developing countries.

Fredskorpset will assist its collaborating partners in exchanging experience, guidance, quality assurance and development in connection with such collaboration.

Structure

Fredskorpset is a public body with special powers. It is accountable to the Foreign Ministry and while it performs its mission in an independent fashion, important questions of principle that arise in the course of its work are decided by the Foreign Ministry. Fredskorpset is led by a board and a secretary-general. Day-to-day operations are managed by a secretariat led by the secretary-general. Fredskorpset has a volunteer service executive committee, consisting of representatives of its partners, which advises the board on Fredskorpset's operations.

Funding

Fredskorpset receives its appropriations via a separate chapter of the state budget.

The Fredskorpset Governance Programme

Fredskorpset and IDASA's Centre for Governance in Africa

Democracy and governance: "Thinking Africa in the Renaissance"

The Centre for Governance in Africa works in conjunction with Fredskopset to facilitate an exchange programme for researchers in Africa. The objective of the exchange programme is to expose young professionals working in the area of governance to political processes in African countries. The secondary objective is to develop a collaboration framework for African-based democracy and governance centres.

The programme aims to achieve the following:
- Facilitate the creation of an enabling environment for nurturing a new generation of leaders with a Pan African outlook;
- Provide an opportunity for governance and democracy non-governmental organisations (NGOs) or non-state actors to engage in the processes of political integration in Africa;
- Nurture and strengthen shared democratic values and principles;
- Help promote and strengthen national, sub-regional and continental democracy and governance.

Key activities include:

- The annual exchange of six researchers among partner institutions dealing with governance and democracy;
- The exchange of information;
- Documentation/publication of research produced by participants; and
- Knowledge creation on best practices and experiences.

The programme was launched in 2004 and personnel from the following organisations have been exchanged:

- The Institute for Democracy in South Africa (IDASA) – lead agency – South Africa;
- The East African Legislative Assembly – Arusha, Tanzania;
- The Southern African Development Community (SADC);
- The Parliamentary and Public Support Trust (PAPST) – Zimbabwe;
- The Centre for Democracy and Development (CDD) – Nigeria;
- The Centre for Development and Democracy (CDD) – Ghana.

The 2004–2005 exchange programme

Name	Home organisation (from)	Host organisation (to)
P. Mutai	East African Legislative Assembly	IDASA
G. Mapani	PAPST	IDASA
P. Ntshongwana	IDASA	Pan African Parliament
T. Matsheza	IDASA	IDASA – Nigeria office
R. Oforiwa	CDD-Ghana	SADC-PF – Namibia
S. Onyengubula	CDD-Nigeria	IDASA-SA

The key partner organisations in the second exchange programme include the following:

- IDASA – lead agency – South Africa;
- Governance, Advocacy and Communications Centre (GAC) – Uganda;
- PAPST – Zimbabwe;
- The Transformation Resources Centre (TRC) – Lesotho;
- CDD – Ghana;
- The Institute for Policy Interaction (IPI) – Malawi.

The 2005–2006 exchange programme

Name	Home Organisation (from)	Host organisation (to)
L. Boakye	CDD – Ghana	IDASA
B. Andinda	GAC	IDASA
T. Madikhetla	IDASA	IPI
S. Masamvu	PAPST	IPI
C. Chilimba	IPI	PAPST
F. Faku	TRC	CDD – Ghana

Highlights and successes

In the 2004-2006 exchange programmes, the participant from Ghana, Regina Oforiwa, was attached to the SADC's Parliamentary Forum. Under its tutelage she was introduced to the concept of gender mainstreaming, gender relations and capacity-building programmes for women parliamentarians and is now applying her skills in West Africa where her organisation is organising capacity-building programmes for Members of Parliament in Ghana.

Glen Mapani from PAPST in Zimbabwe was attached to IDASA. During his tenure he was exposed to administration systems in an NGO, democracy tracking and citizen participation in governance processes. Upon his return to Zimbabwe, Glen introduced new accounting and administrative systems. He is currently studying at the University of Cape Town. Sonny Onyengubula from CDD – Nigeria was attached to IDASA. He is now working with the United Nations in Eritrea on issues of transitional justice. Phakama Ntshongwana was attached to the Pan African Parliament where she collected information and produced information packs for community radio stations on the Pan African Parliament. She also organised round-table meetings to disseminate information about the Pan African Parliament to the public. She is now a researcher at Oxford University. Phillip Mutai from the East African Legislative Assembly was attached to IDASA and taught research methods in governance. He worked closely with the manager of IDASA's Public Opinion Service on baseline surveys to measure the perceptions of citizens on democratic practices. Phillip is now back in East Africa and applying his research knowledge.

In the 2005/06 exchange programme, Sylvester Masamvu from PAPST, Zimbabwe was attached to the IPI. During his tenure he was given the task of linking civil society organisations with the National Assembly. His responsibilities included attending all parliamentary sessions in Malawi and disseminating information on key policy issues to Malawian civil society organisations. Sylvester has been approached by one of the foreign donor organisations in Malawi to stay in the country to manage a capacity-building project for the National Assembly of Malawi.

Bruce Andinda from GAC, Uganda was attached to IDASA. While his key function was to undertake research for IDASA, he also trained researchers in Zambia for a baseline survey, analysed the data and helped produce a plan of action for civil society organisations and parliament in Uganda. He also observed the Ugandan elections and will introduce the concept of public hearings in his own country on his return. Tiisetso Madikezela from IDASA was attached to the IPI in Malawi producing radio programmes for citizens on policy issues in that country. She is currently working with the IDASA's Local Government Centre producing similar programmes.

New programme area

With the current increase in the number of conflicts in Africa, IDASA, in conjunction with Fredskorpset, will introduce a new component to the governance programme – facilitating the exchange of personnel from conflict-ridden areas to countries that are relatively peaceful and stable so that they can be exposed to institutions that deal with conflict resolution. This addition to the governance programme arises from our understanding that stable democracies are dependent on peace and stability. To this end, IDASA has commissioned research to map out conflicts in Africa.

Lessons learnt to date

The exchange programme has been an eye-opener for all the participants. They have all reported that it has shown up their lack of knowledge about socio-political systems in other African countries. All the participants reported that Africa is not one unit; it is not homogenous and that there is a lot to learn from each other.

All the participants also reported that democratic practices vary from one African country to another and they found that in some African countries cultural and traditional practices are deeply entrenched in political systems while in others the Western model of democracy is very prominent. They all agreed that the exchange programme was very beneficial and should be extended to Francophone and Arabic African countries.

For further information contact:

Paul Graham, Executive Director of IDASA, at pgraham@idasa.org.za, Monica Makaula at monica@idasact.org.za or Tanya Shanker at tanya@idasact.org.za

Lyn Chiwandamira
Manager, Centre for Governance in Africa, IDASA

Understanding armed conflict and peace-building in Africa

Lilah Fearnely and Lyn Chiwandamira

Introduction

This chapter is designed to give an introductory overview of conflict analysis and resolution efforts in Africa. It provides a map of current armed conflicts in Africa and an introduction to some of the main theories and frameworks for understanding and dealing with conflict. The paper gives background information to conflicts in Africa and is meant to assist researchers under the Fredskorpset Programme to understand the issues pertaining to conflicts in Africa. The paper draws from the presentations made at a Fredskorpset workshop in Pretoria at the IDASA offices in February 2006.

Understanding conflict

Defining conflict

Conflict can be defined as 'the pursuit of incompatible goals by different groups'.[1] Commentators often distinguish between 'social conflict', which refers to conflict between groups, and 'political conflict', when the nature of the incompatibility is political. Conflict can be further categorised as non-violent and violent. Non-violent conflict is expressed without the use of force and is seen by many as a natural element in human society and an essential driving force for social change. Violent conflict, on the other hand, poses a threat to society and, it can be argued, represents one of the central causes of poverty and 'failed development'.

The focus of this chapter is restricted to violent or armed conflict. A conflict can be categorised as violent when force is used by one or more parties. Violent conflict can include one-sided violence such as genocide[2] against civilians and can range from a single attack on a civilian to full-scale war.[3] An armed conflict is defined as a situation where both parties resort to the use of armed force, in the form of manufactured weapons or sticks, stones, fire, water, etc.[4] Violent or armed conflict is categorised as interstate when waged between governments and intrastate when it occurs within a country between a government and a non-governmental party. The Department of Peace and Conflict Research at Uppsala University further differentiates between intrastate conflicts that are waged with or without the involvement of foreign troops. They use the category intrastate with foreign involvement to refer to an armed conflict in which one or more of the warring parties receive troop support from an outside government.

Most definitions of armed conflict tend to focus on the number of battle-related deaths. The Uppsala Peace and Conflict Research Department defines an armed conflict as: "a contested incompatibility that concerns government and/or territory where the use of armed force between two parties, of which at least one is the government of a state, results in at least 25 battle-related deaths in one calendar year".[5]

Other scholars have preferred to look at the cumulative number of battle-related deaths. For example, Marshall and Gurr (2005) only consider episodes of political violence that have reached a minimum threshold of 1 000 battle-related deaths to be major armed conflicts. Maill et al (2005) also use the cumulative indicator of 1 000 or more battle-related deaths in defining major armed conflicts.

However, accurately measuring battle-related deaths in chaotic conflict conditions can be problematical. Even if we assume that the statistics are accurate, judging the severity of a conflict based on the number of battle-related deaths can be tricky for a number of reasons. First, in many of today's wars civilian casualties outnumber those of combatants and second, the knock-on effects of armed conflict, including malnutrition, lack of access to health care, increased incidences of sexual violence and forced displacement, are not captured in this approach. Thus, while the battle-related deaths indicator provides a useful starting point, it should be support by detailed case-by-case analysis which incorporates information from a wide range of sources.

Armed conflict in Africa

As discussed above, there is much debate regarding the relevance and reliability of statistics that measure armed conflict in terms of battle-related deaths. However, in order to gain an overview of the current level of armed conflict in Africa, the cumulative battle-related deaths indicator provides a useful starting point.

Marshall and Gurr's (2005) Peace and Conflict ledger incorporates data from 161 countries in the world with a population greater than 500 000 in 2005. The ledger highlights those countries with a very real threat of major armed conflict being fought in 2005. In the authors' analysis, episodes of political violence must have reached 1 000 battle-related deaths to be considered an armed conflict.

Figure 1 on the next page provides a visual representation of Marshall and Gurr's analysis in relation to armed conflict in Africa. Black indicates an ongoing (low, medium or high intensity) major armed conflict in early 2005 and grey indicates either sporadic or low intensity armed conflict, in the same period, or an armed conflict that was suspended or suppressed between early 2001 and early 2005.

The overview of the continent as a whole, illustrated in figure 1, helps us to build a picture of regional conflict dynamics. Scholars and practitioners in the field of armed conflict have observed that internal wars invariably have external effects. Regional conflict diffusion or 'overspill' can result from the spread of weaponry, refugee flows, when ethnic groups straddle borders or when non-state armed actors operate from neighbouring countries.[6] In this respect, the level of stability in a country can have serious implications for its neighbours. Thus, in dealing with armed conflict in Africa it is essential to combine country-specific analysis with an understanding of regional conflict dynamics.

The International Crisis Group (ICG) notes that, in Uganda the Lord's Resistance Army's (LRA's) strategy of ambushing humanitarian vehicles and crossing into neighbouring countries has seriously disrupted the peace process in Sudan and the Democratic Republic of Congo (DRC).[7] Another area of regional conflict

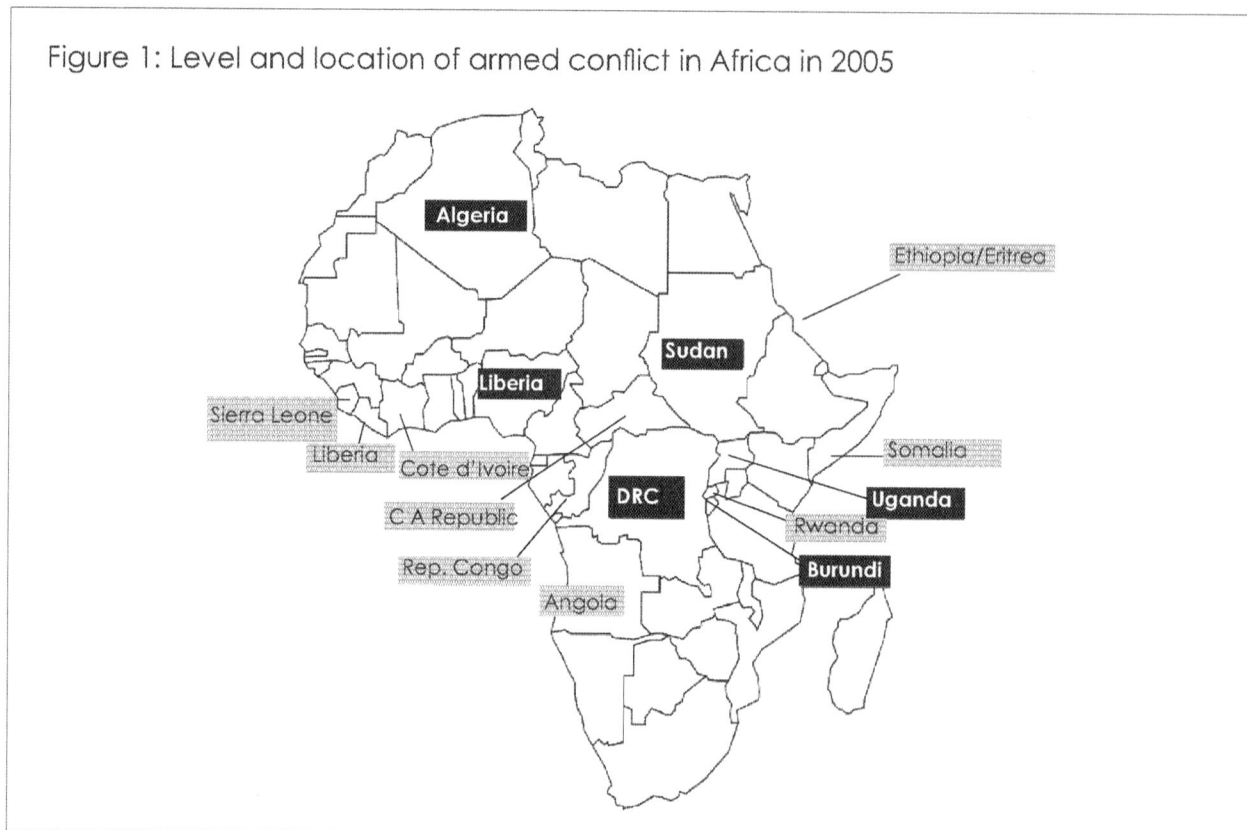

Figure 1: Level and location of armed conflict in Africa in 2005

Source: Marshall and Gurr, 2005

diffusion includes Sudan/Chad. Human Rights Watch (HRW) have highlighted the grave implications of the crisis in the Darfur region of Sudan on neighbouring Chad. The organisation notes that in the past three years there have been attacks on both Chadian villagers and Darfurian refugees, as part of cross-border raids by the Sudanese 'Janjaweed' militias.[8] These are not isolated cases, nor is regional conflict diffusion new. For example, Maill et al (2005) note the phenomenon of regional conflict spillover in the Great Lakes area and West Africa during the immediate post-Cold War period.[9]

However, considering regional dynamics is significant when analysing not only factors that precipitate conflict but also those that generate peace. For example, many analysts believe recent developments in Liberia, including the democratic elections that installed Ellen Johnson-Sirleaf as President, could have positive repercussions for West Africa as a whole. The ICG note that "Just as Liberia once dragged its neighbours into a horrific war, it could now – with good policy and strong donor support – become an anchor for stability in Sierra Leone, Guinea and Côte d'Ivoire".[10]

Refugees and internally displaced persons in Africa

As noted in earlier sections, it is important to look beyond the 'battle-related death' indicator in order to gain a more nuanced view of the level and dynamics of armed conflict. Statistics that capture the flow of refugees and internally displaced persons (IDPs) provide a useful source of information both in terms of assessing the level of armed conflict as well as the 'spillover effects' and possible implications for neighbouring countries. The United Nations High Commissioner for Refugees (UNHCR) is a good place to start. Figure 2 illustrates the top five refugee-producing countries in Africa as well as the main countries of asylum. Figure 3 shows the five countries with the highest IDP populations in Africa at the time of writing.

Figure 2: Origin of major refugee populations in Africa – 2004

Country of origin	Main countries of asylum	Total
Sudan	Chad, Uganda, Ethiopia, Kenya, DRC, Central African Republic	730 600
Burundi	Tanzania, DRC, Rwanda, South Africa, Canada	485 800
DRC	Tanzania, Zambia, Congo, Burundi, Rwanda	462 200
Somalia	Kenya, Yemen, United Kingdom, USA, Djibouti	389 300
Liberia	Guinea, Côte d'Ivoire, Sierra Leone, Ghana, USA	335 500

Source: UNHCR, 2005

Figure 3: IDPs in Africa – 2006

Country	Latest IDP figure
Sudan	5 355 000
Uganda	1 740 498
DRC	1 664 000
Algeria	1 000 000
Zimbabwe	569 685

Source: Internal Displacement Monitoring Centre, 2006

Root causes of conflict

It is widely accepted that understanding and addressing the root cause of a conflict is essential to a successful and lasting resolution. While there is no unified theory on the cause of violent conflict, there are a number of factors that have been cited as explanations.

The observation that 'lesser developed' countries tend to experience higher levels of violent conflict has led some scholars to assume a causal link between poverty and war. However, it now widely accepted that poverty per se does not cause conflict. Structural inequality – that is, economic and social inequality and unequal access to political power – is considered one of the central causes of violent conflict. While some analysts focus on differing group identities such as ethnicity, religion or economic class as sources of conflict, others view identity as an idiom through which other interests are expressed.

Other factors that have been cited in the propensity to conflict include the relationship between military expenditure and economic growth (a debate located within the field of development economics) and the prevalence of small arms, which has been highlighted by think-tanks such as Saferworld. The scarcity or abundance of natural resources as well as the role of economic agendas have been explored by a number of scholars.

Some analysts locate the origins of violent conflict in the broader historical or development processes and look at issues such as state formation in the post-colonial era or the role of rapid market-orientated economic reforms such as structural adjustment policies in generating instability and violent conflict in turn.[11] More recently commentators have started to look at issues such as unequal trade relationships between 'developed' and 'developing' countries and the role this plays in generating economic decline and violent conflict.[12]

There is rarely a single cause of armed conflict; rather there are multiple causes, conditions and contingent factors that cause social conflict to become violent or armed. However, it can be argued that for the purpose of conflict resolution and prevention, it is both necessary and useful to look for the shared characteristics and patterns. Wallace and Jung (2002) use the 1998 European Council definition of 'root causes' of conflict (page 7) as a useful working definition. This approach can then be supported by a detailed country/region-specific analysis.

Root causes of conflict (European Council Definition, 1998)

1. Imbalance of political, socio-economic or cultural opportunities among different ethnic groups, including socio-economic inequalities, exclusive government elites, violation of political group rights, destabilisation by refugees and internally displaced people and other demographic pressures.

2. Lack of democratic legitimacy and effectiveness of governance, including a legitimacy deficit of government and public institutions, insufficient or declining public services, criminality, social and political violence, and biased law application and enforcement by justice and security services.

3. Absence of opportunities for the peaceful conciliation of group interests and for bridging dividing lines between different identity groups. This includes absence of effective dispute resolution mechanisms, absence of pluralism/diversified debate, distrust among identity groups and weak or harming external engagement.

4. Lack of an active and organised civil society, including weak civil society organisations, absence of professional and independent media and lack of economic 'peace interests'.

Source: Wallace and Jung, 2002

Conflict mapping

There are multiple causes and dynamics in every conflict. Meaningful peace building and conflict resolution must start with a detailed analysis of the causes of conflict and the specific conditions of a certain country or region. Conflict mapping and analysis is the first step towards understanding and managing conflict. Maill et al (2005) suggest using the following framework, based on Weher's (1979) guidelines for initial conflict analysis as a practical starting point.

Conflict mapping template (based on Weher's 1979 guidelines)

A: Background
1. Map of the area
2. Brief description of the country
3. Outline of the history of the conflict

B: The conflict parties and issues
1. Who are the core conflict parties? What are the internal subgroups and on what constituencies do they depend?
2. What are the conflict issues? Is it possible to distinguish between positions, interests (material interests, values, relationships) and needs?
3. What are the relationships between conflict parties? Are there qualitative and quantitative asymmetries?
4. What are the different perception of the causes and the nature of the conflict among the conflict parties?
5. What is the current behaviour of the parties (is the conflict in an escalatory or de-escalatory phase)?
6. Who are the leaders of the parties? At elite/individual level, what are their objectives, policies and interests, and relative strengths and weaknesses?

C: The context: global, regional and state-level factors
1. At the state level: is the nature of the state contested? How open and accessible is the state apparatus? Are there institutions or fora which could serve as legitimate channels for managing the conflict? How even is economic development and are there economic policies which can have a positive impact?
2. At regional level: how do relations with neighbouring states and societies affect the conflict? Do parties have external regional supporters? Which regional actors might be trusted by the parties?
3. At the global level: are there outside geopolitical interests in the conflict? What are the external factors that fuel the conflict and what might change them?

Source: Maill et al, 2005

Gender and armed conflict

There is increasing recognition of the gendered nature of violent conflict and the need to address the 'invisibility' of women and girls in this area. The United Nations Security Council Resolution 1325 on women, peace and security, adopted in October 2000, addresses the impact of armed conflict on women as well as their undervalued contribution to conflict prevention and peace-building.[13]

In unstable and chaotic conflict and 'post-conflict' situations, women and girls are often the victims of sexual violence including systematic rape as well as forced recruitment into armed movements and into sexual slavery. As Amnesty International notes: "When political tensions degenerate into outright conflict, all forms of violence increase, including rape and other forms of sexual violence against women".[14] Amnesty International's report, which covers 131 countries across the world, highlights some examples of the impact of armed conflict on women in Africa. The gravest include systematic gang rape of women and young girls by the Janjaweed militia in Darfur, Sudan and rape committed by armed groups as well as UN forces in the DRC.[15]

However, women are not simply passive victims. Women have played active roles as both combatants and commanders, as well as being a driving force for peace, reconstruction and reconciliation. Despite the increasing recognition of the importance of mainstreaming gender into work on peace and security, women remain to a large degree invisible. This invisibility manifests itself in their exclusion from high-level peace negotiations and post-conflict power structures. It has also been argued that women's contribution to early warning has been undervalued, deterring conflict prevention initiatives.

In order to address the invisibility of women and girls as both victims and actors in armed conflict it is essential to devise strategies for gender-sensitive peace-building and post-conflict reconstruction, as well as considering the role of women in early warning. This means women having an "equitable presence at peace negotiations as well as in legislature and in the planning and operation of humanitarian interventions and peace-keeping missions. It has also been recommended that international Truth and Reconciliation Commissions be set-up to highlight the plight of female war victims".[16]

The role of women soldiers must also be addressed in the war-to-peace transition. Female ex-combatants face different challenges from those of their male counterparts. Stereotypical notions of gender-appropriate work and behaviour are often re-mobilised in the war to peace transition. This can lead to the exclusion of female ex-combatants from re-insertion programmes as well as their failure to register due to social stigma. It has been noted that:

> There are few easy solutions for women who have been soldiers in wars in Africa. Assistance programs must first of all be aware that female ex-soldiers do exist, and then seek them out. To help these women on their way towards reintegration – if not within their original community, then somewhere else of their choosing – is a great challenge. Reintegration planners must also pay special attention to disabled women (and girl) veterans.[17]

Dealing with armed conflict

Terminology[18]

Commentators and practitioners have noted that the terminology used in relation to handling violent or armed conflict tends to be inconsistent. For the sake of clarity, the following section provides a brief definition of some of the most widely used terms. It should be noted that the list is not exhaustive and usage tends to vary from one analyst to another.

Conflict resolution

A widely used yet ambiguous term. It incorporates work that addresses and resolves the root causes of conflict. It is used both in reference to the intention to carry out the above activities as well as the completion of the process.

Peace enforcement

The imposition of a settlement by a powerful third party.

Peace-keeping (and peace support operations)

Used generically to refer to UN and other regional body missions and operations that fall short of military combat. Peace-keeping has evolved from a focus on simply containing and stabilising the situation until negotiations produce a lasting peace agreement, to an expansion of activities including human rights monitoring, demobilisation activities, policing and temporary administration.[19]

Peace-building

Refers to the full spectrum of intervention that is focused on restoring relations between groups that have been in conflict. As such, peace-building involves several different aspects, which may include forgiveness, cooperation, negotiation, mediation, facilitation, creation of mutual understanding and/or reconciliation.

Track 1 diplomacy

Works from the top down and occurs between heads of state, other political figures and intergovernmental representatives. Track 1 diplomacy uses formal negotiations in an attempt to reach political agreements (peace agreements, ceasefire agreements, etc.).

Track 2 diplomacy

Also top down, but it usually involves unofficial mid-level leaders from international NGOs, churches, academics and private business. It is often used as a supplement or precursor to track 1 diplomacy.

Track 3 diplomacy

Works from the bottom up. It involves activity at grassroots level attempting to form and heal relationships between ordinary citizens in conflict areas.

Conflict resolution

There are varying approaches to conflict resolution. Some of these approaches are summarised below in a presentation given by Professor Prof Dirk Kotzé (UNISA) at an IDASA/Fredskorpset workshop on peace and conflict resolution held in February 2006.

Different contending approaches to conflict resolution

Conflict resolution can be studied from several different perspectives or approaches. The following are only a number of them:

1. Traditional methods of conflict resolution: *gacaca* (Rwanda), *kgotla* (Botswana), *barza* (DRC). More focus is placed on these methods and more research is done in this area.

2. Islamic approach to conflict resolution (Mali). Since 9/11 more sensitivity exists in Muslim communities about negative stereotypes and associations with terrorism. Paul Salem (American University, Beirut) has done important research work in this area.

3. Legal or judicial approach, especially the emphasis on transitional justice. It involves the use of truth commissions and criminal tribunals or special courts, and also the

---

relationship between conflict/conflict resolution and public international law (especially international human rights law and international humanitarian law).

4. The institutional focus on the African Union: institutions like the early warning system, Standby-force and the Peace and Security Council are also a focus for research.

5. The reconciliation and state-building paradigm – discussed below.

6. Stabilisation and consolidation of peace paradigm – discussed below.

7. Terrorism as a focus area – more in terms of multilateral cooperation than domestic conflict and policies; some countries have adopted legislation in this respect

8. Sociological approach: focus on women, child soldiers, refugees and IDPs in conflict.

Reconciliation and state-building paradigm

Used by the South African government and Institute for Democracy and Electoral Assistance (IDEA): Paradigm is democratisation + economic development. Can also refer to it as an institutional or constitutional approach. It also includes the democratic peace paradigm. The paradigm consists of the following:

1. Facilitation or mediation by eminent persons or Presidents: Nyerere, Mandela (Burundi), Masire (DRC), Moi (Sudan), Kiplagat (Somalia), Obasanjo and Mbeki on behalf of the AU (Darfur, Côte d'Ivoire, etc).

2. Shuttle diplomacy, especially to negotiate a ceasefire with the rebel movements.

3. Dialogue to decide on the transition: Sun City (DRC), Naivasha and Machakos (Sudan).

4. Negotiating a peace agreement (comprehensive peace agreement/global and inclusive accord).

5. Two-phase constitution-making: first an interim constitution and then a final constitution, linked by an election.

6. A transitional package consisting of:

   • Government of National Unity;

   • Truth commission;

   • Integration of armed forces and demobilisation, disarmament and reintegration (DDR);

   • Formation of commissions for human rights, election management, media, judicial services, etc.

Stabilisation and consolidation of peace paradigm

This paradigm is implicit in the approaches of the African Union (AU) and in Côte d'Ivoire. It consists of:

1. Predominantly a military/security focus.

2. Concentrate on involvement of UN and AU in humanitarian assistance and peace-keeping.

3. Introduce concept of 'post-conflict reconstruction' – example Sudan, Angola and Mozambique.

4. The deficiencies of this paradigm are captured in the new concept of 'developmental peace missions'.

Terrorism (associated with the 'clash of civilisations' paradigm)

1. Involves mainly the AU and local law enforcement agencies + intelligence.

2. It is more international in character than a domestic or African issue.

Galtung's influential model, in which he notes that conflict can be viewed as a triangle with contradiction (i.e. causes) at the top and behaviour and attitudes at the bottom corners, is illustrated below. The figure shows which aspects of conflict are dealt with by which type of intervention. Causes (perceived or real) of incompatibility can be addressed through peace-building. The attitudes of the conflict parties – in other words their perceptions of each other – can be tackled through peace-making. Finally, behaviour, which may include threats and attacks, is tackled through peace-keeping.[20]

Figure 4: Galtung's conflict triangle

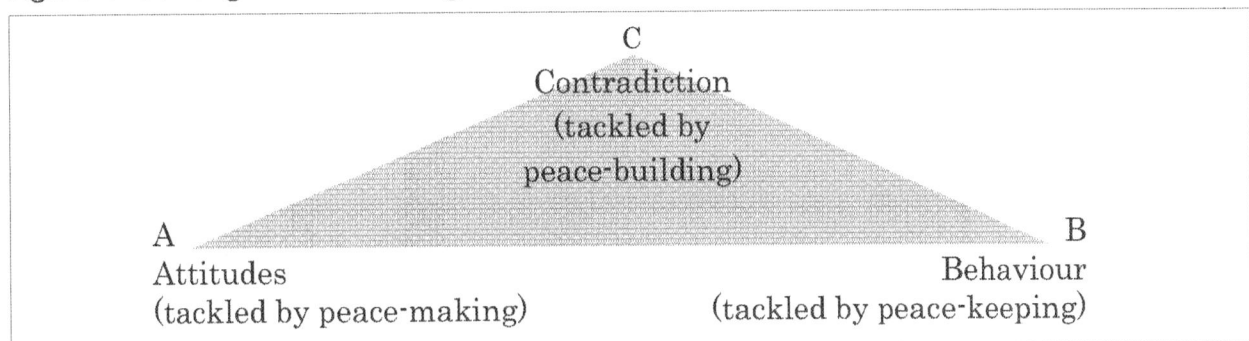

C
Contradiction
(tackled by
peace-building)

A
Attitudes
(tackled by peace-making)

B
Behaviour
(tackled by peace-keeping)

Source: Galtung, 1969

Peace-keeping in Africa

Peace-keeping missions tend to represent the first stage, in terms of top down interventions, in dealing with armed conflict. Peace-keeping missions' aim is to stabilise the situation until negotiations produce a lasting peace agreement. In the past, peace-keeping missions have tended to be the preserve of the United Nations, with African countries contributing 'blue helmet' troops to missions. In recent years there has been much discussion on the need to increase African capacity to deal with armed conflict in a self-sufficient manner. Much of the debate has focused on the AU and its role in current and future peace-keeping missions on the continent. There has some been progress towards this end, including the establishment of the AU-led mission in Sudan (AMIS) and moves towards developing the African Stand-by Force which aims to provide "equal distribution of labour on peace-keeping among the nations".[21] A detailed discussion of peace-keeping in Africa is provided in the April 2005 edition of Conflict Trends, available through the website of the African Centre for the Constructive Resolution of Disputes (ACCORD).

Figure 5 shows African peace-keeping missions at the time of writing. For further details on each of the missions see ACCORD's Conflict Trends issue on peace-keeping.[22] Up-to date information on UN peace-keeping missions in Africa is available through the UN website.[23]

Figure 5: Current African peace-keeping missions

MONUC	DRC
UNAMSIL	Sierra Leone
UNMIL	Liberia
UNOCI	Côte d'Ivoire
ONUB	Burundi
UNMIS	Sudan (Southern)
UNMEE	Ethiopia and Eritrea
AMIS	Sudan (Darfur)

Source: ACCORD, *Conflict Trends*, 2005

Democracy, democratisation and conflict

Democratisation is often promoted by the 'international community' as a sure-fire means of consolidating peace. It is based upon the observation that democracies do not go to war. It has led to the common assumption that democracy should be introduced as soon as possible. Some analysts have been critical of this 'one-size fits all' approach and argue that it is essential to critically examine the relationship between democracy, democratisation and violent conflict.

While the issue of democratisation in the aftermath of armed conflict is highly complex, it still considered by many to be an essential element in consolidating peace. It has been argued that "despite many trials and tribulations with democracy in today's multiethnic societies, no other form of government – including non-democratic power sharing, party-based authoritarian control, rule by the military, or the overwhelming force of a dictatorship – can more effectively reconcile competing social interests. For this reason, understanding how types and practices of democracy may contribute to or help exacerbate intractable conflict is a critical concern".[24] Organisations such as the Electoral Institute of Southern Africa (EISA) address such issues through their programme on conflict management, democracy and electoral education, details of which are available via their website.

Preventing armed conflict

There is an increasing recognition among practitioners and policy-makers that more energy and resources should be dedicated to preventing armed conflict. Conflict prevention aims to address root causes and escalating factors.

Conflict prevention "aims both to prevent or impede violence and destructive conflict and to build a just and sustainable peace by transforming underlying 'latent' causes of conflict".[25]

The 1999 Carnegie Commission Report on Preventing Deadly Conflict played a significant role in increasing the focus on operational (immediate) and structural (root causes) conflict prevention. These concepts were later adopted by the international community and have become a cornerstone for thinking on conflict prevention. The African Centre for the Constructive Resolution of Disputes and many other NGOs have devoted significant energy to conflict prevention over a number of years. More recently, the forging of civil society networks, such as the Global Partnership for the Prevention of Armed Conflict (GPPAC), is testament the shift in focus from reaction to prevention.

The GPPAC was formed in response to the recommendations of UN Secretary-

General Kofi Annan in his report on the Prevention of Armed Conflict (2001), in which he called for NGOs with an interest in conflict prevention to organise at international level. The GPPAC initiator organisations for the African region include the West Africa Network for Peace Building (WANEP), the Nairobi Peace Initiative–Africa (NPI) and ACCORD.[26]

Early warning is considered by some analysts as essential to conflict prevention. It has been described as "any information from any source about escalatory developments, be they slow and gradual or quick and sudden, far enough in advance in order for a national government, or international or regional organisation to react timely and effectively, if possible still leaving them time to employ preventative diplomacy and other non-coercive and non-military preventative measures".[27] The potential role of women in early warning and the importance of gender mainstreaming within UN conflict prevention has been a particularly interesting development to the debate.

Other analysts stress the importance of conflict-sensitive development. Development and humanitarian assistance can create or fuel conflict. Saferworld notes that "certain large-scale irrigation systems in Africa, rather than helping to build prosperity, have only served to deepen conflicts between local communities over access to water" and argues that development programmes should be informed by "a thorough understanding of the actual and potential causes of violence".[28] The role of aid in supporting peace or fuelling conflict is discussed in work such as Mary Anderson's analysis, do no harm.[29]

Notes

1   Maill et al, 2005.

2   Article 2 of the 1948 UN Convention on Genocide defines the term as meaning any of the following acts committed with intent to destroy, in whole or in part, a national, ethnic, racial or religious group:

   (a)   Killing members of the group;

   (b)   Causing serious bodily or mental harm to members of the group;

   (c)   Deliberately inflicting on the group conditions of life calculated to bring about its physical destruction in whole or in part;

   (d)   Imposing measures intended to prevent births within the group;

   (e)   Forcibly transferring children of the group to another group.

3   Maill et al, 2005.

4   Definition of arms from Uppsala Conflict Data Project of the Department of Peace and Conflict Research of Uppsala University.

5   http://www.pcr.uu.se/database/index.php

6   Maill et al, 2005.

7   International Crisis Group, 2006a.

8   Human Rights Watch, 2006.

9   Maill et al, 2005, p. 80.

10   International Crisis Group, 2006b.

11   See for example, Storey, A. 1999.

12   See chapter on trade and conflict (p. 21) in Saferworld and International Alert, 2004.

13   UN Resolution 1325, October 31 2000

14   Amnesty International, 2005

15   Amnesty International, 2005

16   UNIFEM, 2003.

17   Barth, E. 2003.

18   Definitions based on Maill et al 2005 and Mtimkulu, B. 2005

19   Mtimkulu, B. 2005.

20   See Maill et al 2005, Wallace and Jung, 2002.

21   Mtimkulu, B. 2005, p. 34

22   For information via ACCORD on African peace-keeping missions visit, http://www.accord.org.za/ct/2005-4.htm

23   For detailed information on UN peace-keeping missions visit http://www.un.org/Depts/dpko/dpko/index.asp

24   Sisk, T. 2003.

25   Barnes, C. 2003.

26   Details can be found in the resources and further reading section.

27   Hill, F. 2003.

28   Saferworld, section on conflict-sensitive development available via website http://www.saferworld.org.uk/en/csd_uganda.html

29   Anderson, M. 1999.

Resources for further reading

On-line, general

ACCORD, http://www.accord.org.za/

ACCORD, An International Review of Peace Initiatives (Published by Conciliation Resources), http://www.c-r.org/accord/index.htm

Africa Peace Forum (APFO), http://www.amaniafrika.org/

Centre for the Study of Violence and Reconciliation (Johannesburg), http://www. wits.ac.za/csvr/

Centre for Conflict Resolution (University of Cape Town), http://ccrweb.ccr.uct. ac.za/

International Peace Academy (IPA), http://www.ipacademy.org/

International Alert, http:// www.international-alert.org/

International Crisis Group, http://www.icg.org

Journal of Humanitarian Assistance, http://www.jha.ac

Journal of Conflict Resolution, http://www.library.yale.edu/un/un2f1a1.htm

Nairobi Peace Initiative – Africa (NPI-Africa), http://www.npi-africa.org

Online Journal of Peace and Conflict Resolution, http://www.trinstitute.org/ojpcr/

Relief web, http://www.reliefweb.int/w/rwb.nsf

West Africa Network for Peacebuilding (WANEP), http://www.wanep.org/index1. html

On-line, conflict prevention

Global Partnership for the Prevention of Armed Conflict, http://www.gppac.net/

Forum on Early Warning and Early Response (FEWER), http://www.fewer.org/

On-line, refugees and IDPS

United Nations High Commissioner for Refugees, http://wwww.UNHCR.org

Internal Displacement Monitoring Centre, http://www.internal-displacement.org

Forced Migration Review, http://www.fmreview.org/

US Committee for Refugees and Immigrants, http://www.refugees.org

On-line, conflict and democracy

EISA project on Conflict Management, Democracy and Electoral Education (CM-DEE), http://www.eisa.org.za/index.html

International Institute for Democracy and Electoral Assistance, http://www.idea.int/

On-line, gender, armed conflict and peace

Peacewomen, http://www.peacewomen.org/

UNIFEM Portal on Gender, Peace and Conflict, http://www.womenwarpeace.org/

Books

European Centre for Conflict Prevention. 1999. Searching for peace in Africa,

Utrecht, Netherlands

Jentleson, Bruce (ed). 2000. Opportunities missed, opportunities seized, Maryland: Rowman and Littlefield

Lund, Michael. 1997. Preventing violent conflict, Washington: USIP Press

Prince, Thomas. 1995. Intermediaries in international conflict, New Jersey: Princeton University Press

Ury, Bill. 1999. Getting to peace, New York: Viking Press

References

Anderson, Mary B. 1999. Do no harm: How aid can support peace – or war, Boulder, Colorado: Lynne Rienner Publishers Inc.

Amnesty International. 2005. Responsibilities have no borders, http://t2web.amnesty.r3h.net/report2005/intro-index-eng.

Barnes, C. 2003. Living document on civil society and conflict prevention, European Centre for Conflict Prevention/CSP International Secretariat.

Barth, E. 2003. The reintegration of female soldiers in post-conflict societies, Aid Workers Exchange, http://aidworkers.net/exchange/20030820.html.

Carnegie Commission on Preventing Deadly Conflict. 1997. Preventing deadly conflict: Executive summary of the final report. New York: Carnegie Corporation of New York.

Department of Peace and Conflict Research, University of Uppsala, Conflict database, http://www.pcr.uu.se/database/index.php.

Ekiya, T. 2006. A practitioner's analysis of current gaps in implementing UN Security Council Resolution 1325, available via the Centre for Conflict Resolution website, http://ccrweb.ccr.uct.ac.za/

Galtung, Johan. 1969. 'Violence, peace and peace research', in Journal of Peace Research 3, pp.167–192.

Hill, F. 2003. 'The elusive role of women in early warning and conflict prevention', in ACCORD, Conflict Trends, 3/2003, issue on women, peace and security, pp.11–17.

Human Rights Watch. 2006. Report on Chad, www.hrw.org/backgrounder/africa/chad0206/1.htm.

International Crisis Group. 2006a. 'A strategy for ending Northern Uganda's crisis', Africa Briefing, 35.

International Crisis Group. 2006b. 'Liberia: Staying focused', Africa Briefing, 36, 13 January 2006.

Internal Displacement Monitoring Centre, 2006. www.internal-displacement.org/

Mtimkulu, B. 2005. www.accord.org.za/ct/2005-4/ct4_2005_pgs34_36.pdf—'The African Union and peace support operations', in ACCORD, Conflict Trends, 4/2005, Focus on peace-keeping, pp.34–36.

Marshall, M. and Gurr, T. 2005. A global survey of armed conflicts, self-determination movements and democracy, University of Maryland, College Park: Center for International Development and Conflict Management.

Maill, H., Ramsbotham, O. and Woodhouse, T. 2005. Contemporary conflict resolution. The prevention, management and transformation of deadly conflicts. Cambridge: Polity Press.

Sisk, Timothy. 2003. 'Democracy and conflict management', in Burgess, Guy and Burgess, Heidi, Beyond intractability, Boulder, Colorado: Conflict Research Consortium, University of Colorado, USA. www.beyondintractability.org/essay/democ_con_manag/

Saferworld and International Alert. 2004. Strengthening global security through addressing the root causes of conflict: Priorities for the Irish and Dutch Presidencies in 2004.

Storey, Andy. 1999. 'Economics and ethnic conflict: Structural adjustment in Rwanda', Development Policy Review, 17, pp.43–63.

Thakur, R. 2005. 'From peace-keeping to peace operations', in ACCORD, Conflict Trends, 4/2005, Focus on peace-keeping, pp.3–9.

UNHCR. 2005. Refugees by numbers.

UNIFEM. 2003. 'Women, war and peace', in ACCORD, Conflict Trends, 3/2003, issue on women, peace and security.

United Nations. 1948. Convention on the Prevention and Punishment of the Crime of Genocide, www.hrweb.org/legal/genocide.html

United Nations. 2000. UN Council Resolution 1325, October 31 2000.

Wallace, T. and Jung, M. 2002. Enhancing UK capacity for handling conflict: The rationale for a UK civilian peace service, Peace Workers UK, www.peaceworkers.org.uk/researchpage.html

Regional integration in Africa

Implications for parliamentary practices and procedures

Michael Mataure

Introduction

Many parliamentarians in Africa have, since the time of their countries' independence, followed variations of their former colonisers in Western Europe in terms of the conduct of business and general procedures. Indeed, the mode of dress and actual seating arrangements in the former British colonies were to a large extent modelled on those of the United Kingdom's parliament at Westminster. On the other hand, the national assemblies of the francophone African countries tended to emulate the Assembly Nationale in France.

Parliamentary practices and procedures in Africa can therefore be described as a mixture of foreign conventions, traditions and culture given the fact that many countries have been independent for less than 40 years.

Indeed, there are efforts to reform and indigenise those behaviours and norms of conduct which are aggregated into practices and procedures that are commonly referred to as the Standing Rules and Orders of Parliament and are printed in a legislature's rulebook.

As highlighted in other chapters, there are many challenges that are related to the strategy of bringing about integration in Africa in the areas of governance and democratisation. In the case of parliaments and national assemblies in Africa, these challenges manifest themselves in a number of ways. Some are the result of the particular country's history and its subsequent evolution into a parliamentary democracy, albeit in its very early stages of development.

Challenges

1. The first and most common of these is the function and perceived/assumed role of the institution as one of the three arms of government. It is the commonly held belief and convention that a house of representatives has three main roles: a representative role, a legislative role and an oversight role.

   While this is the case, there is limited understanding of these and related responsibilities and obligations within the national context and even less so at the level of the electorate. For the larger population, their honourable Member of Parliament (MP) is the chief development agent, the individual who will bring their health facility to within walking distance and provide coffins when their relatives die, to name only a few of the expectations. In their eyes, their MP is their main representative and general functionary. It therefore is critical that this individual has access to abundant resources in all forms: financial and material as well as human. The attendant attributes of the MP should, of necessity, include patience, accessibility, listening capacity and unlimited time.

2. There is also limited appreciation among the electorate and other stakeholders of the relationship that should exist between the executive and legislative branches of state. This is probably the most challenging in the arrangements around the operations of government. Often it is this particular relationship that creates most difficulty in the governance process of the state.

3. Parliaments and national assemblies in Africa often cite lack of adequate resources for their failure to meet regularly and conduct business, including scrutinising and reviewing the executive and its policies and programmes. In many countries the sitting calendars and sessions of the legislature are under

the total control of the executive. This branch of state is also responsible for determining the level of appropriation within the budget of parliament as well as when to release or withhold funding. Clearly, the control of the institution's budget by the executive compromises a legislature's independence and effectiveness, especially in carrying out the essential functions of oversight, representation and legislating.

4.   Further misunderstanding often arises because the roles and functions of the political parties are also not clearly appreciated. For the most part governing parties and their members treat the bureaucracy of state, i.e. the civil service, as an extension of their organisation. This also applies to access to and use of state assets, facilities and resources (human, financial and material) both during campaigns and in day-to-day situations.

5.   There is also limited appreciation of the need for the separation of powers among the three arms of government and often this results in conflict. This is particularly evident in cases where a dominant governing party holding a significant number of seats in parliament forms a government. The house of representatives is then regarded as an extension of the executive and is not expected to question, challenge or scrutinise the decisions and actions of the executive in any meaningful manner but to act more as a rubber stamp.

6.   MPs are often unable to consult their constituents on a regular basis due to limitations of human, financial and technical resources. This leaves them in an unfortunate and undesirable situation where they make decisions and vote on matters with little or no input from their electors. Representation is therefore significantly compromised and the mandate of the people rendered immaterial.

7.   It is worth noting that the existence of diverse political opinions between governing and opposition parties has tended to render the working relations within parliaments adversarial and in some extreme cases totally untenable. There is such polarisation during campaigns and after elections that debates and consensus are not possible even on issues that are in the national interest and for which a partisan view would be detrimental to the cause at hand. This particular point is critical since most matters in parliament are decided by way of vote, whether in the enactment of legislation or the ratification of an international convention or protocol.

8.   The legislative framework which provides for parliament's existence includes the country's constitution and electoral laws and any special statutory instruments and regulations (including the Standing Rules and Orders) need to be

harmonised to provide adequate guidelines for parliament's efficient and effective operation. In many cases, the existing legal instruments and provisions are subjected to political interference and manipulation and are even disregarded by apparently powerful individuals, often protecting political and personal interests.

The points raised above provide an insight into the operating environment for many parliaments and national assemblies in Africa. The list is by no means exhaustive but it does provide the main areas that impact directly on the smooth operation and administration of a legislature in the African setting. The autonomy and resourcing which would enable a parliament to be truly effective and responsive to the needs of the electorate can only come about through an evolutionary process that has been agreed to by all principal and secondary stakeholders.

The issues raised above have profound impact on the ability of a parliament to work in tandem with both regional and eventually continental integration initiatives. Ultimately there is a need to generate consensus and a sense of ownership among those in authority in a given country, such that there is sufficient political will to advance the cause.

What, then, are the implications for parliamentary practices and procedures in the context of regional integration in Africa?

What issues need to be addressed on the road towards regional integration? Integration is intended to provide harmonisation and the development of the critical mass of countries working for the common good, welfare and sustainable transformation of Africa to assume its rightful place in the world.

1. First and foremost there must targeted and focused efforts to genuinely empower parliaments through appropriate statutory provisions and compliance with the same. These must provide for, among other things, clear separation of powers and sanctions for non-adherence.

2. Parliaments must be provided with adequate human, financial and material resources to be able to exercise their cardinal functions, which includes supporting elected members to play their primary roles of representation, legislating and oversight of the executive.

3. There must be genuine efforts to ensure that political parties do not interfere with the operations of parliament and those of the bureaucrats of state. This should include safeguarding the rights of ordinary citizens in every aspect, including holding diverse political views and opinions.

4. The issue of domestication and localisation of international and regional conventions must be addressed. Protocols and charters require that a certain capacity be developed to expedite these processes. Furthermore, there should be processes in place to ensure that there is the requisite political will and buy-in at the critical levels. This will ensure that ratification and harmonisation in the local context is not an administrative ritual but becomes a reality.

5. There should be consultation and participation of a country's citizens to the extent that is practically possible if the matters are to be part and parcel of what impacts on their rights and freedoms.

Relations between East African Legislative Assembly and Pan African Parliament

Kenneth Madete

Introduction

In 1999, Kenya, Uganda and Tanzania signed the Treaty of East African Cooperation as the culmination of a process of negotiations initiated in 1993. In part motivated by shared history and benefits that the region had enjoyed from cooperation until 1977 when the old community collapsed, the East African Community (EAC) is also seen as a mechanism for dealing with the current challenge of development of the peoples of the region in the context of globalisation and international competition. Thus, the vision of the EAC is very much rooted in the present and its goal is an improved standard of living for East Africans, through progressive deepening and broadening of regional integration in social, economic and political dimensions.

The Treaty for the establishment of the EAC allows for the creation of organs and other institutions of the EAC, one of which is the East African Legislative Assembly (EALA). The EALA is the independent legislative arm of the EAC. Its other organs are the Summit, which is composed of the three heads of state, the Council of Ministers composed mainly of ministers responsible for regional cooperation, the East African Court of Justice, the Coordination Committee, sectoral committees, the Secretariat and other such organs as may be established by the Summit.

The three heads of state formally inaugurated the EALA on 30 November 2001. It had its first sitting in Arusha, Tanzania on 29 November 2001 at which the Hon. Abdulrahman O. Kinana, an elected member from Tanzania, was unanimously elected Speaker.

Political structure

There are 27 elected members of the EALA, nine from each partner state and five ex-officio members. Members are indirectly elected in the sense that they are elected by their respective national assemblies, although not from within the ranks of the national assembly itself. In the formula adopted in the Treaty, it is required that the members so elected represent a diversity of views in their national assemblies as well being representative in terms of gender. Women's representation varies from country to country, for example Kenya has two women members and Tanzania three.

The five ex-officio members comprise three ministers, one from each partner state, who are responsible for regional cooperation, as well as the Secretary General and the counsel to the EAC.

Functions and mandate

The Treaty bestows upon the EALA the legislative function of the EAC. Like most legislatures, the EALA has the following major functions:
- To liaise with the national assemblies of partner states on matters relating to the EAC;
- To debate and approve the budget of the EAC;
- To consider annual reports on the activities of the EAC, annual audit reports of the Audit Commission and any other reports referred to it by the Council of Ministers;
- To discuss all matters pertaining to the EAC and make recommendations to the

council as it may deem necessary for the implementation of the Treaty;

- To establish any committee or committees for the purpose of carrying out its functions as it deems necessary;
- To recommend to the Council of Ministers the appointment of the clerk and other officers of the assembly;
- To make its own rules of procedure and those of its committees; and
- To perform any other functions as are conferred upon it by the Treaty.

As the legislative arm of the EAC, with oversight functions on all matters that fall within the EAC's work, the assembly has a very wide remit. This is reflected in the scope of the mandate of the standing committees that handle the substantive work of the assembly.

As the elected representative of the people of East Africa, the assembly has recognised the role it can play in linking the EAC and its governance organs with the peoples of East Africa. To this end, it has visited various parts of East Africa to publicise the EAC and its work and to familiarise itself with the conditions, resources and challenges of the people of region.

EALA and the Pan African Parliament

The Treaty obliges the EAC to foster co-operative arrangements with other regional and international organisations whose activities have a bearing on the EAC's objectives. The Treaty specifically mentions the African Union (AU), to whose objectives the African Economic Community regional organisations are expected to contribute under the Lagos Plan of Action.

Under the relevant provisions of the Treaty Establishing the African Economic Community, the EAC has submitted its application for accreditation as a regional economic community to the commission of the AU.

At the initiative of the Speaker of the EALA the regional parliaments were, however, initially allowed by the steering committee for the establishment of the Pan African Parliament (PAP) to participate at the sessions of the PAP as observers. The final decision, of course, now lies with the PAP itself and other policy-making organs of the AU.

Article 18 of the protocol to the Treaty Establishing the African Economic Community defines the relationships between the PAP and the parliaments of the regional economic communities. It states:

> The Pan African Parliament shall work in close co-operation with
> Parliaments of the Regional Economic Communities and the Na-

tional Parliaments or other deliberative organs of Member States. To this effect, the Pan-African Parliament *may*, in accordance with its Rules of Procedure, convene annual consultative fora with the Parliaments of Regional Economic Communities and the National Parliaments or other deliberative organs to discuss matters of common interest.

The word "may" does not make it mandatory for the PAP to convene these annual consultative fora, but it leaves it to the PAP's discretion.

The fourth paragraph in the preamble of the protocol relating to the establishment of the PAP notes that, as a vision, "the Pan-African Parliament is to provide a common platform for African peoples and their grass-roots organisations to be more involved in discussions and decision-making on the problems and challenges facing the continent".

The last paragraph further states that the member states are "firmly convinced that the establishment of the Pan African Parliament will effectively ensure the full participation of the African peoples in the economic development and integration of the continent".

During its first term of existence, the PAP will exercise advisory and consultative powers only. Moreover, if all countries were to ratify the Constitutive Act establishing the AU, the protocol establishing the AU and ultimately the protocol establishing the PAP, the maximum membership of this body would be 265 for a continent of over 700 million people, or one MP for over 2.64 million people. This falls way short of one of the core functions of any parliament, that of effective representation of its people.

The position of the EALA is that the consultative fora mentioned above are essential and their scope should be clearly defined in the rules of procedure of the PAP. The PAP needs, and must constantly liaise with, regional and national parliaments in order to create effective links in the development of relevant programmes, and to establish mechanisms of forging common positions on issues relating to the New African Partnership on Development (NEPAD), the New Africa Initiative and the fast globalising world.

Until membership is by universal adult suffrage and at a ratio more meaningful to the principle of representative democracy, the need for the PAP to have constant and regular consultations with regional and national parliaments and other deliberative organs requires no further elaboration.

Bruce Andinda

Country study: Uganda

Bruce Andinda is a research officer for the Governance and Communication Centre (GAC - Uganda). His duties include data analysis, report writing and logistics support.

Editor's note — Bruce Andinda wrote this chapter some time before the parliamentary and presidential elections held in February 2006. Where resulting political events and political changes within part d the Ugandan leadership have necessitated the updating of this report, this has been done. Otherwise, the analysis reported here remains intact, and its focus is still on the 2005 referendum, as envisaged by the author.

The referendum process in Uganda

Bruce Andinda

Uganda is in East Africa and is bordered by Kenya in the east, Sudan in the north, the Democratic Republic of Congo in the west, Rwanda in the southwest and Tanzania in the south. The southern part of the country includes a substantial portion of Lake Victoria, within which Uganda shares borders with Kenya and Tanzania. Uganda takes its name from the historical Buganda kingdom, which encompasses a portion of the south of the country including the capital, Kampala. The country has a population of approximately 27 million people.

History

Little is known about the history of the region now covered by Uganda until the arrival of the Arabs and Europeans in the mid-1800s. People are known to have lived in the area since at least the first millennium BC.

When Arabs and Europeans arrived in the 19th century they encountered a number of kingdoms, including those of Ankole, Buganda, Bunyoro, Busoga and Toro. The largest of these was Buganda which is part of Uganda today. Islam and

Christianity were introduced to these kingdoms.

The area was placed under the charter of the British East Africa Company in 1888 and was ruled as a protectorate by the United Kingdom from 1894. Several other territories and chiefdoms were integrated and the protectorate took its final shape in 1914.

By 1966, the first prime minister, Milton Obote, had overthrown the constitution and declared himself president, ushering in an era of coups and counter-coups that lasted until the mid-1980s. In 1971, Idi Amin took power and ruled the country with the military for the next decade.

Idi Amin's rule cost the lives of an estimated 300 000 Ugandans and he forcibly removed the entrepreneurial East Indian minority from Uganda, thereby decimating the economy. His reign ended in 1979 after an invasion by Tanzanian forces aided by Ugandan exiles. The situation improved little with the return of Milton Obote, who was deposed once more in 1985.

The current president, Yoweri Museveni, has been in power since 1986 and was viewed as being part of a new generation of African leaders. However, there is controversy about his influence, under which the Ugandan Constitution was changed to accommodate life presidency. The changing of the Constitution allowed him to return for a third term after 20 years in power.

Stability has been brought to the country with the exception of Northern Uganda, which continues to struggle with a rebel insurgency.

Politics

Executive

The executive is headed by Museveni, who is both head of state and head of the armed forces. The president is elected by a popular vote for a five-year term. The last presidential and parliamentary elections were held in February 2006. The president appoints the vice-president, prime minister and the ministers who aid him in achieving his tasks.

Judiciary

The Ugandan judiciary operates as an independent branch of government and consists of the magistrates' courts, high courts, court of appeals and the supreme court. High court judges are appointed by the president and approved by the legislature.

Legislature

The parliament is formed by the national assembly, which has 303 members. Of these, 214 are directly elected and the remainder are nominated by legally established special-interest groups, such as those for women, the army, youth, disabled people and labour. Members are elected for five-year terms.

In a measure ostensibly designed to reduce sectarian violence, from 1986 political parties have been restricted in their activities. In the non-party "movement" system instituted by Museveni when he came to power in that year, political parties continued to exist but could not campaign in elections or field candidates directly (although electoral candidates could belong to political parties).

Uganda multiparty referendum, 2005

Ugandans voted to restore a multiparty political system in a constitutional referendum held on 28 July 2005. (Five years ago, in a similar referendum, Ugandans chose to keep the restrictions on the parties.) Enthusiasm for the poll was muted, however, as both the government and opposition supported a return to a multiparty system. Some political groupings, including the Forum for Democratic Change (FDC), boycotted the poll, claiming that it would legitimise 19 years of rule by an effective one-party state. President Museveni castigated the boycotters for "not contributing to the development of Uganda". Other observers suggested the $12.5m spent on the referendum might have been put to better use elsewhere in Uganda, one of the poorest countries in the world.

The lengthy question presented to voters on their ballots was criticised for being confusing: "Do you agree to open up the political space to allow those who wish to join different organisations/parties to do so to compete for political power?" Symbols of a tree and a house accompanied the "yes" and "no" boxes, respectively, on the ballot papers.

More than 90% of those who voted backed the return to multiparty politics. Some observers expressed surprise at the official voter turnout figures. Initial estimates indicated that less than 30% of Uganda's 8.5 million voters had turned out for the poll. The Electoral Commission, however, released an official figure of 47%. (See table on pg 35.) A low turnout would have been a big embarrassment for President Museveni so the official figures shown by the Electoral Commission were regarded as highly dubious by election observers.

The referendum process that was carried out in July 2005 did not achieve its goals simply because it was regarded as an avenue to misuse taxpayers' money and people were not interested in participating in it. This is one of the reasons for the low turnout.

The figures in the table below are based on final results published by the Ugandan Electoral Commission for 99.9% of polling stations.

Registered voters	8,524,230	
Option	**Number of votes**	**Percentage**
Yes	3 643 223	92.4
No	297 865	7.6
Turnout	3 941 088	47.3

Uganda is now a multiparty state with seven major political parties: the National Resistance Movement (NRM), FDC, Democratic Party (DP), Uganda People's Congress (UPC), Justice Forum (JEEMA), Conservative Party (CP) and Free Movement Party (TFM). President Museveni, who was eligible to contest the multiparty presidential elections as president of the NRM since the term limits for presidents were removed, was returned to power. However, the main opposition party, the FDC, challenged the election results, citing widespread irregularities and fraud. Former exile, Kizza Besigye, head of the FDC, who came second in the presidential poll, unsuccessfully petitioned the Supreme Court.

Louis Boakye

Country study: Ghana

Louis Boakye is a parliamentary liaison officer at the Ghana Centre for Democratic Development (CDD-Ghana). His duties include management of committees of parliament that examine financial and economic bills, agreements, loans, taxes, budgets, and state finances.

Editor's note – In his efforts to assess the state of governance in Ghana Louis Boakye examines the government's legislature, judiciary and executive and touches on issues such as corruption, civil society involvement, freedom of speech and corporate governance. His conclusion poses the question: are there signs of deepening democracy in that country.

The state of governance in Ghana

Louis Boakye

Introduction

Ghana is a West African country of approximately 18.8 million people, sharing borders with Ivory Coast in the west, Togo in the east and Burkina Faso to the north and bordering the Atlantic Ocean in the south. It is a democratic country with an independent executive, legislature and judiciary. Political leaders are elected every four years through general elections based on universal adult suffrage.

Ghana gained independence from the British in 1957 and became a republic in 1960. Kwame Nkrumah of the Convention People's Party (CPP) became the country's first president. The history of government in Ghana has been marked by military coups in 1966, 1972, 1978 and 1979. The 1979 coup was led by Flight Lt. Jerry Rawlings and the Armed Forces Revolutionary Council (AFRC). Although a civilian administration was installed, it was overthrown again by Rawlings and his Provisional National Defence Council (PNDC) in 1981. Eleven years of military rule followed until multiparty elections were held in 1993. This election was won by Rawlings who remained in power as president until 2001 when elections were won by John Agyekum Kufuor of the New Patriotic Party (NPP), Ghana's current president. President Kufuor also won the 2004 elections for his second and final term.

Currently, Ghana has a hybrid system of governance combining elements of both the presidential and parliamentary systems. There is an executive president and a bi-partisan legislature.

Both the president and members of parliament are elected through multiparty elections.

Politics

The legislature

Ghana's present parliament consists of 230 elected members without any appointees. It is a unicameral legislature headed by a Speaker. Currently, the ruling NPP has 128 members, the National Democratic Congress has 94, the People's National Convention has four, the CPP has three and there is one independent member. Of these 230 members, 25 (representing 10.87%) are women.

The president, the vice president and ministers of state who are not members of parliament can attend and participate in its proceedings but cannot vote.

As it stands now, there is some fusion between the executive and the legislature as the Constitution enjoins the president to appoint the majority of ministers from parliament. This means some members of the legislature (MPs) are also ministers of state (members of the executive branch) at the same time. Also, bills that are passed by parliament require presidential assent before they become law.

Civic participation in and engagement with the legislative process is increasing, even though some legal constraints have yet to be shed. For example, the Standing Orders of Parliament generally presume all committee meetings are closed to the public unless the committee decides that a specific meeting shall be held in public. Even then, the chairman of a committee has the power to eject all "strangers" from a committee meeting at any point.

Despite these difficulties, parliament's consultation with civil society organisations (CSOs) and the public at large on key issues seems to be becoming an accepted feature of Ghana's current democratic dispensation.

The judiciary

There is also an independent judiciary headed by the Chief Justice (currently Justice George Kingsley Acquah). The highest court of the land is the Supreme Court which mainly considers constitutional interpretations. Below the Supreme Court are the Appeals Court, the High Court, magistrates' courts and circuit courts.

Justices of the superior courts are appointed by the president with the prior approval of parliament. However, the president cannot dismiss a judge. By and large, the judiciary appears independent of the other branches of government as evidenced by the fact that the government has lost a host of high-profile cases.

Equality, availability and accessibility of justice still remain a challenge. Some cases remain pending for years, especially cases that involve litigation on land issues. These delays, coupled with the cost of court charges and the cost of hiring lawyers, force many people, especially the poor, to shun the use of the judicial system for the settlement of grievances.

Though the judicial system remains effective, its lack of efficiency is a drawback. There is also a public perception of corruption among some members of the judiciary. This has prompted the current Chief Justice to embark on series of programmes to curb the corruption. Senior judges and a court registrar have been prosecuted for corruption.

The executive

The executive branch of government is headed by the president who appoints ministers to help him execute his duties. President Kufuor has no military background and was the first opposition presidential candidate to come to power by winning an election against an incumbent party. He lives a humble life and operates a government that seemingly listens to the voice of the people. President Kufuor occasionally meets members of the press to explain his government's policies and actions. He has also instituted a concept called "the People's Assembly" in which he interacts with and answer questions directly from members of the general public once a year. Assemblies are also held in each district (i.e. at local government level) to benefit the people at the grassroots.

The "Meet the Press Series" involves ministers meeting the press periodically to answer questions and clarify issues pertaining to their sectors.

Ghana was also one of the first two African countries to submit themselves to the peer review mechanism under the New Partnership for African Development initiative.

Local governance

Ghana has three spheres or levels of government: national, regional and district. The national government is headed by the president. Each of the ten regions (provinces) is headed by a regional minister who is appointed by the president with the approval of parliament. Each region is further divided into districts (municipalities) with each district headed by a district chief executive who is appointed by the president with the approval of a two-thirds majority vote of the district assemblies.

The district assembly is the main grassroots level of government. Assembly members are elected from all towns, suburbs and villages to constitute a district assembly (i.e. a miniature parliament at local level), with the president appointing a further 30% of members. District assemblies are responsible for every government function at district level. About 7% of annual national revenue is distributed to the district assemblies as a common fund. Apart from the common fund, each district collects its own additional revenue through local taxes and levies.

Corruption

A major challenge that confronts the current government is the issue of corruption. Studies conducted by independent bodies, including the Ghana Center for Democratic Development, have shown that the majority of the people perceive the government to be corrupt. Transparency International's assessment of Ghana has also indicated a rise in the perception of the level of corruption. Ghana was ranked 65 out of 159 countries surveyed by Transparency International and included in the 2005 Corruption Perception Index Report. Out of a maximum score of 10, Ghana scored only 3.5, compared to 3.6 in 2004.

Civil society involvement

Civil society and the media remain very strong and alert. Democratic activism is very high. CSOs strive to affect legislation, governance and public administration in all dimensions. CSOs also champion the cause of the poor and the vulnerable, such as disabled people, orphans and alleged witches.

On the whole, the ability of CSOs to influence national policy decisions remains high.

Freedom of speech and media freedom

Free speech and media freedom were enhanced by the repeal of the criminal libel law in 2001. Journalists are now free to practise their profession without fear of being put behind bars. Some journalists, however, are abusing this freedom and producing unfounded stories about politicians and reputable people. This has led to heavy fines being imposed on some media houses after being found guilty of civil libel by the courts.

Another problem is the domination of politics in the media. The print and the electronic media seem to have gone politics crazy as about 80% of their space/air-time is devoted to politics.

Corporate governance

Corporate governance and labour relations in Ghana still remains volatile with labour unions frequently embarking on strike action, despite legislation to stop the phenomenon. Most strikes have been by health and educational workers. Expatriate employers have also often been accused of violating the rights and dignity of their local employees and this has also contributed to strikes and protest in the private sector.

Proposed changes to electoral laws

At the time of writing, the government had introduced the Representation of the People's Amendment Bill in parliament, which would make it possible for every Ghanaian living anywhere to register and vote in all public elections and referenda.

Until then, one must be resident in Ghana to register and vote. Of those abroad only those who are on official duties are allowed to vote, including officials of Ghana missions and their families, security personnel on peacekeeping operations, officials of the UN and students on government scholarships.

The government believes that the current law, which was passed by the previous regime, discriminates against Ghanaians abroad who do not fall within the definition of "official duties", hence the introduction of the Amendment Bill to ensure that all Ghanaians abroad get equal treatment. The government also argues that this will be in accordance with the letter and spirit of the constitution, which says that "Every citizen of Ghana above 18 years of age and of sound mind" has the right to be registered for the purposes of public elections and referenda.

As the former ruling party that passed the existing law, the main opposition party, the NDC, strongly opposes the Amendment Bill. The opposition says government is introducing this law to entrench itself in power. It says government would like to account for its dwindling domestic support by roping in the votes of people outside the country who may not know the poverty and hardships facing people on the streets.

The opposition also argues that there are no available statistics on the number of Ghanaians abroad, which will make it impossible to determine how many are eligible to vote.

The independent electoral commission does not have the resources and the capacity to extend its work and services to all countries in which Ghanaians presently reside.

The opposition also argues that ambassadors and heads of Ghana missions abroad would serve as returning officers (election officers) and, since most of these people are political appointees, their independence and fairness cannot be assured. Furthermore, since Ghana does not have embassies/missions in all countries where there are Ghanaians, the new law will still be discriminatory.

These arguments for and against the Amendment Bill generated a lot of tension and divided people along party lines. The NDC boycotted the proceedings of the Parliamentary Committee on Constitutional, Legal and Parliamentary Affairs that was tasked to consider and report on the Bill to parliament. The committee has held discussions and public forums on the Bill in all ten regions of Ghana. It has also moved to other countries to collect the views of Ghanaians there.

Ghanaians are very anxious about the outcome of this Bill. At any open forum where this Bill has been mentioned, tensions have usually risen very high and debate raged in the Ghanaian media and in political circles.

Conclusion

Democracy seems to be deepening in Ghana. More and more people openly discuss politics and matters of governance with the overwhelming majority expressing preference for the current multiparty form of governance rather than one-party rule or military dictatorship. Civil society is becoming stronger on issues of governance and democracy. However, the economic well-being of Ghanaians and corruption remain problems for the current democratic dispensation. As the majority of Ghanaians perceive the current government to be corrupt, it must do more to enhance its integrity and reduce corruption.

Tiisetso Madikhetla

Country study: Malawi

At the time of writing, Tiisetso Madikhetla was an intern presenter and producer at IDASA. Her responsibilities included conducting interviews and assisting in writing the organisation's electronic newsletter.

Editor's note – Tiisetso Madikhetla writes about three events that she observed and participated in while serving as an FK scholar at the Institute for Policy Interaction (IPI) in Malawi; a workshop conducted by the Catholic Commission for Justice and Peace (CCJP), in partnership with the IPI, for Members of Parliament (MPs) where they were informed what their constituents had to say about their leadership, based on research conducted by the CCJP at grassroots level; the IPI's "Right to Livelihood" economic empowerment programme; and a workshop for the Parliamentary Women's Caucus and civil society organisations aimed at building bridges between these groups and helping them develop effective channels of communication. Her observations and descriptions are situated within the context of her overriding interest – the role that the media can play in empowering citizens in a way that enables them to participate actively in politics.

Media and civil society: A catalyst for change in Malawi

Tiisetso Madikhetla

Background

Malawi has a population of about 12.9 million with 90% of the population living in rural areas. The ethnic groups that make up the Malawian population include the Chewa, Nyanja, Yao, Tumbuka, Lomwe, Sena, Tonga, Ngoni and Ngonde, and there are small minorities of Asian and white people. The Chewa or Chichewa, the largest group, live largely in the central and southern parts of the country. The Yao are found predominately around the southern area of Lake Malawi. Tumbuka are based mainly in the north of the country and the Asians and whites live mainly in the cities.

In working with the Institute for Policy Interaction (IPI) it became clear to me that the media in Malawi can be a catalyst for change in communities. It can help establish a spirit of cooperation within communities which can encourage citizen participation in politics, economic development, good governance and accountability. It enhances citizenry empowerment, erasing misperceptions in communities and enabling citizens to make informed decisions. This is the underlying theme of this chapter.

Workshop on vertical accountability and responsiveness

The Catholic Commission for Justice and Peace (CCJP), in partnership with the IPI, conducted a workshop in which Members of Parliament (MPs) were told what their constituents had to say about their leadership. The CCJP had conducted research at grassroots level to investigate the lack of communication between MPs and their constituents. People did not have a clear understanding of the role of councillors and MPs, nor of the importance of service delivery, transparency and participation in community projects, and they had to learn about the dangers of relying on handouts.

The CCJP interviewed members of about 25 constituencies in the south of the country, all of whom lived in remote rural areas. Participants were a mix of people from the CCJP parish committees and ordinary residents. The research found that out of the 25 constituencies, only five MPs lived in the areas they represented; the remainder stayed in the cities of Blantyre and Lilongwe. The CCJP study also showed that :

1. Eight MPs out of the 25 constituencies have not addressed a public meeting since they were elected, and seven only addressed the public after the election to thank residents for voting them into power;

2. Most constituents do not know what their MPs are doing; only two MPs consult their constituencies before going to parliament. The rest make no effort to consult with their constituencies, choosing instead to hold discussions with traditional authorities;

3. A total of 17 MPs don't have offices in the constituency where they can meet with their constituents. Some may use their own house, if they live in the area, or that of a relative, or the premises of the constituency chairperson. Most MPs don't have constituency offices;

4. The relationship between MPs and their constituents is shrouded in misunderstanding. Some MPs have even resigned without informing their constituencies.

As a result, the constituents have lost their trust and confidence in their elected leaders;

5. The CCJP also noted a tense relationship between MPs and councillors. In recent years, MPs and councillors have competed against each other, with the councillors usually the losers. This is exacerbated when they come from different political parties, which is often the case, and when there is a lack of clarity about their respective roles and responsibilities;

6. Tension also arises when councillors hold meetings that MPs are unaware of.

7. MPs tend to disregard councillors as unimportant, and when councillors are not paid salaries, MPs believe jealousy arises.

This results in conflict and uncertainty in the public participation sphere. Miscommunication between the public and elected leaders leave communities struggling to get their needs met or services delivered. In the majority of constituencies, MPs and councillors extend handouts whenever they can, with the result that people come to expect this and at public meetings they make demands for allowances, making meaningful participation difficult. When allowances and handouts are not forthcoming, the leaders are rejected as incompetent.

In parliament MPs are more likely to vote according to their own interests, for example on salary increases, while issues of concern to civil society receive less attention.

Also critical to the issue of representation is the fact that Malawian cabinet ministers are generally recruited from among the legislators, but this is not an absolute requirement and non-elected technocrats can become ministers. Between 1999 and 2004 a number of MPs were interviewed about the issue of "doubling" ie performing the roles of MP and minister simultaneously. It was concluded that it is often impossible for an individual to properly perform the duties of both a minister and an MP. In many cases, MPs neglect their constituencies because their ministerial duties are so demanding. In addition, as ministers they are required to serve the entire country, while in their role as MPs they must serve only their constituency.

During the workshop, an IPI drama group performed a play called 'tiyeni tigwirane manja' or 'let's join hands'. In this drama, constituents met with their village chief to request that councillors and MPs be discharged from their duties because they were not delivering on the promises they had made during their election campaigns. The play depicted MPs' and councillors' lack of loyalty to the constituents who voted for them. In a later scene, MPs and councillors, both with different roles to play, learn to work closely with the chief, especially on development projects.

The drama demonstrated that consultation is essential if MPs are to effectively present their constituents' plans or issues to parliament. It also showed that civil matters can best be solved if MPs, councillors, rural communities and chiefs work together. The wide gap between the citizenry and MPs needs to be closed and accountability must be enhanced so that MPs and councillors are able to reach agreement with people on development projects through a process of dialogue.

This is where the media has a role to play as a mouthpiece of civil society, educating the public to actively participate in democratic processes, regardless of their political ties. Civic journalism can help people overcome their feelings of powerlessness and isolation.

There are further strategies that can be used to reach underprivileged constituencies in order to empower them so that they can participate in the governance process:

1. Local organisational capacity – civil society activists must organise communities to work together and mobilise resources to make their voices heard and ensure their demands are met;
2. Accountability – state officials and public and private employers must be held accountable for their policies, actions and use of funds;
3. Participation – participation in decision-making is vital to ensure that the limited public resources are used in accordance with local needs and wants;
4. Access to information – on the whole, an informed society is able to take advantage of opportunities and access services, exercise its rights and hold the state and non-state parties accountable. However, Malawi's ruling party has used politics as a tool or mechanism to intimidate the opposition.

Economic empowerment in Malawi

Since Malawi moved from being a one-party state to a multiparty state in 1993, there have been some reforms; labour issues and labour law in particular appear to have undergone some changes. However, these changes are not a true reflection of what is still going on in practice in the labour sector. In the tea, coffee and tobacco estates unfair working condition are rife and companies continue to withhold pertinent information on their rights from their employees.

In 2004, the IPI implemented a project entitled the "Right to Livelihood" in the Phalombe, Mulanje, Thyolo, Zomba and Kasungu districts, which aimed to educate people about labour rights. The project sought to sensitise tobacco, tea and coffee estate workers, as well as general labourers in other sectors, to their rights. Some estate workers earn less than MK 1000 (R50) a month and some workers are paid in second-hand clothing or food instead of money.

IPI also conducted research on tenancy labour and found that the majority of people, especially those in the rural areas, don't know about their rights as workers and tenancy has become equated with slavery. At the time, the Executive Director of IPI, Rafiq Hajat, told a leading Malawian newspaper that the IPI's initiative was to educate people in the affected areas about their employment rights and labour laws. In other words, the idea was to empower employees to make informed decisions whenever they encountered employment issues.

As part of this initiative, the IPI produced a free Employment Record Book to be distributed to workers, especially those in the rural areas, through district labour offices, district commissioners' offices and Blantyre and Lilongwe labour offices. This book is to help employees and employers keep track of the employees' salaries, and record information needed when disputes arise between employers and employees. Labour officers working in the field reported to the IPI that workers complained they are sometimes not paid for months, that they receive food or old clothes instead of money, and that they are not granted maternity leave.

In Phase One of the project, the IPI went out into the field to inform and educate estate workers about their rights. They told workers that they have the right to a minimum salary according to the Employment Act and that they are entitled to reasonable working hours. IPI's drama group performed a play about the use of the Employment Record Book. The play was performed in Chichewa, Malawi's national language, to make sure it was properly understood. Its aim was to educate the community about the importance of this book, and labour officers, district commissioners, chiefs, as well as owners of the tea, coffee and tobacco estates were invited to the performance. At the performance IPI Director Rafiq Hajat officially handed over copies of the books to the labour officers.

Thoko Chembe, a labour lawyer who has been working with the IPI on the Right to Livelihood project, elaborated on the 2001 Employment Act, which is printed on the book's cover:
1. Wages should be paid in legal tender and not in kind, for example in clothing;
2. The minimum urban wage is K87.50 per day or K2257 per month and the minimum rural wage is K66.50 per day or K1729,00 per month;
3. A maximum of eight working hours per day is permitted.

In each district that the IPI visited every stakeholder – including members of the community, traditional leaders and government officials – were given Employment Record Books. They were also given the opportunity to question their respective labour officers or the IPI's lawyer about the books.

In my observation, the majority of the population, which is mostly in the rural areas, lacks opportunities to earn a livelihood and there are few employment options. This makes it difficult for people to assert their labour rights. Most estate employees simply sign their employment contracts without reading them or consulting anyone about them. They are terrified that if they delay someone else will get the job. They end up not getting paid or getting paid less – or being given torn clothes and food instead of money.

The situation is getting so bad that Malawians now have to migrate to neighbouring countries, such as South Africa, Zimbabwe, Zambia and others, in search of work. It is usually the men who migrate, leaving their wives and children behind to fend for themselves. According to Hajat, some people search for days for work that in the end pays them very little and offers no certainty of a job the next day. He said that the IPI's "Right to Livelihood" campaign is not a luxury – it seeks improvements to workers' living conditions that are basic human rights.

The IPI's current focus is liaising with estates owners and employers about the availability of the Employment Record Books. The IPI aims to expand the programme in the future to include more workers.

Building bridges between the Parliamentary Women's Caucus and civil society

The IPI held a workshop on Building Bridges Between the Parliamentary Women's Caucus and Civil Society. It was noted that the Caucus and civil society had no communication strategy; they functioned like two trains on separate railway lines that never meet. The workshop aimed to eradicate the negative perceptions each side had of the other and also considered how the media could play a dynamic role in this.

Civil society organisations observed that the Caucus does not properly represent gender issues; it does not play a vocal public role or address gender imbalances in parliament. It also does not promote gender participation in local government and there is no cooperation between the Caucus and civil society organisations in outreach programmes or in research work or consultancy.

On the part of the Caucus, there was the feeling that civil society organisations are always opposed to parliament and the government, that they are donor-driven and that they have political agendas. Furthermore, according to the Caucus, civil society is ill-informed about the challenges facing parliament, as well as about parliamentary proceedings; it uses the media to attack parliamentarians and fails to give praise when it is due,

The media, as the watchdogs and even "guide dogs" of society, were given an opportunity at the workshop to present their views on how communication between the Caucus and civil society can be improved. They suggested that the Parliamentary Women's Caucus and civil society organisations seek allies in the media to promote discussions and actions on issues of concern to them. They also said that the Caucus needed to develop media strategies and liaise with the media. In the workshop it was pointed out that the fact that the Caucus has only one researcher is problematic. It means the Caucus has limited information and therefore is not able to situate gender issues within the bigger picture.

The fact is that the Caucus has limited resources, lacks support from the business community and has insufficient funds, resulting in its failure to implement projects it embarks on.

In conclusion, the IPI recognised that both the Parliamentary Women's Caucus and civil society organisations are part of the same society and both make important contributions to the state.

This workshop, and other IPI initiatives in Malawi, clearly demonstrates that there is a need for programmes that take parliament to the people. The majority of people cannot actively participate in parliament; they see parliament as the palace of politicians. They are only informed by the media if there is major national alert or when parliament holds its first sitting. Thereafter committees don't consult much with the media or civil society about what is happening in parliament.

My point is that there are insufficient media liaison officers, communication officers and researchers in parliament to properly disseminate information to the grassroots level. Parliament, the media and civil society must coexist peacefully and work together to build our democracy.

Simon Fako

Country study: Lesotho

Simon Fako works for the Transformation Resource Centre (TRC) in Lesotho as an Assistant Democracy Educator. His responsibilities include organising youth visits to parliament and training local authorities, chiefs and communities on local government issues. He also organises workshops for local leaders on governance issues.

Democracy and good governance in Lesotho

Simon Fako

Background

Lesotho gained full independence from Great Britain on 4 October 1966. The Kingdom of Lesotho was established as a constitutional monarchy with a bicameral
parliament consisting of a senate and an elected national assembly. In the aftermath of Lesotho's independence, in the period 1966–1970 the country experienced
embryonic democracy. Infant democratic institutions and a rather less conducive
culture of political intolerance marked this period. The period 1970–1986 could be
termed the era of one-party authoritarianism marked mainly by a mixture of Machi-
avellian politics of repression and accommodation. The third period of Lesotho's

governance system, 1986–1993, was characterised by military authoritarianism. This was the climax of undemocratic rule in Lesotho in which political parties were largely banned and the country experienced the most horrendous human rights abuses in its political history. Civil society organisations were also banned. The period 1993–1998 witnessed military withdrawal and the re-institutionalisation of multiparty democracy, marked by turbulence and conflict. The year 1998 saw the birth of a fragile and enfeebled democracy.

Since 1998, Lesotho has made considerable strides in attempting to nurture and consolidate its democracy. The most important steps in this direction are:

1. The peaceful resolution and constructive management of the 1998 violent conflict;
2. A successful negotiation process inclusive of all key stakeholders that facilitated consensus on major agreements and was mediated by South Africa;
3. The establishment of a political structure, styled the Interim Political Authority (IPA), which was able to bridge the wide political divide between the ruling party and opposition parties in the aftermath of the 1998 conflict; and
4. The widely acclaimed, successful electoral reform process that witnessed the replacement of the British style first past the post (FPTP) electoral model by a new, mixed member proportional model after the 2002 general election.

The institutional and legal framework for democratic governance is as critical as the sustenance and viability of democracy itself, for democracy cannot endure if the institutional and legal context is not conducive to such a system. The primary organs of the state are the executive, the legislature and the judiciary. Civil society has a critical role in governance and must claim its rightful space in law making, policy making and policy implementation by government ministries and departments.

Outcome of the 1998 election

The outcome of the 1998 election was one-party rule[1]. The Lesotho Congress for Democracy (LCD) won 61% of the votes but secured 79 seats out of a total of 80 seats in parliament. The Basotho National Party (BNP) won 25% of the votes but secured only one seat. The Maramatlou Freedom Party (MFP) received about 1% of the votes but did not get a single seat in parliament. The main opposition party felt cheated by the ruling party and other parties felt excluded by the system. The opposition parties vented their anger in the streets[2]. What started purely as a political conflict escalated into violent conflict, which drew in the military and nearly sparked a civil war in Lesotho. This situation invited military intervention by Botswana and South Africa. The negotiation process, which was brokered by South Africa on behalf of the Southern Africa Development Community (SADC), delivered a peace settlement involving:

1. The establishment of the IPA to liaise with the government and the Independent Electoral Commission (IEC) in preparing for the next election;
2. The holding of a fresh election sometime in March of the year 2000.

The mode of governance needed to be more inclusive. Representation was to be under either the proportional representation system or at least a mixture of both proportional representation and the FPTP system. This would ensure the relative stability of the political system based upon a multiparty parliament with opposition participating constructively in the process of governance.

Under a different system, the 1998 election would have delivered a different outcome. Either proportional representation or a mixture of proportional representation and the FPTP system would have broadened representation and participation in the political system. An electoral system must act as a conflict resolution mechanism to stabilise the political system and encourage the political elite to engage in politics of consensus, compromise, dialogue and tolerance. Because the 1998 election failed to do this, conflict led to loss of life and property, deepening polarisation of an otherwise homogenous nation.

A debate took place under the auspices of the IPA. An overwhelming preference for a mixed system, which could combine the advantages of proportional representation and the FPTP system, was the result. Electoral reform was advocated as part of the constructive management of Lesotho. Ultimately, through the IPA, it was resolved that Lesotho's electoral model be changed from the British style FPTP to the Mixed Member Proportional Representation (MMP) system. This was the most progressive stride made in Lesotho's political history, aimed at addressing and redressing the entrenched culture of political violence and intolerance. The MMP system was used in the general election of 2002. The results pointed to its enormous prospects for instilling a culture of consensual rather than coercive politics, representative parliament, inclusive governance and accountable government structures.

Key lessons from the Lesotho experience

These are the primary lessons that African countries can learn from the Lesotho experience:

1. The negotiation process: key stakeholders need to be involved. The process involves agreement by the parties that negotiations are necessary. It also involves a common stance to be taken by key actors. The next step is to arrive at a common agreement on the methodology or the modalities of conducting the talks. This should be followed by the actual negotiations and finally the implementation of agreements and common decisions based on a shared agenda of negotiations.

2. Constitutional review process: electoral reform ought to be accompanied by constitutional review.

3. Electoral system reform: Lesotho illustrated the deficiencies of the FPTP system, the most important of which revolve mainly around the following:

   • it tends to produce a minority government (legitimacy deficit);
   • it does not lend itself easily to broad representation of various political forces in the legislature (inclusivity deficit); and
   • it tends to generate, rather than reduce, various types of conflict (stability deficit).

   Electoral reform should be guided by the following criteria:

   • ensuring a representative parliament;
   • making elections accessible and meaningful;
   • providing incentives for conciliation;
   • facilitating stable and efficient government;
   • holding the government and representatives accountable;
   • promoting a parliamentary opposition; and
   • cost and administrative capacity.

4. Managing election-related conflicts. There is a need for flexible approaches in addressing and redressing election-related conflicts and for using mediation to resolve such conflicts. There is a need to establish an electoral tribunal that deals with election disputes speedily.

Regularity of elections

Competitive elections are a hallmark of all democratic systems of government. The central issue in any election is whether the voting and related processes are both secret and transparent. These two criteria are acknowledged worldwide as standards for assessing the conduct of elections as free and fair. Secrecy and transparency are also criteria that confer legitimacy on elected governments. In other words, the authenticity of any regime that has won national elections is reliant on the conditions under which voters cast their ballots.

Lesotho, which has a homogeneous population, is one of the countries that is susceptible to this problem. Every election since independence has been attended by a dispute of some kind. In every case, the outcome has been rejected by the losing political parties on the grounds that the electoral process failed to meet one of the criteria mentioned above. However, Lesotho has been holding its elections regularly since independence in 1966.

Civil society participation

Youth participation

This section focuses on the changing trends and patterns in the youth's participation in promoting good governance and democracy in Lesotho. It examines trends in electoral participation in general and that of the youth in particular and proposes ways of improving youth participation and representation in political life. This, we admit, is a very narrow view of participation as the youth have other modes of political participation: for instance, they get involved in advocacy for changing electoral laws in order to be included in the political arena. The ultimate test of their participation, however, is the extent to which they are able to influence who gets elected, as elections provide an important opportunity for the electorate to express their preferences on the policies and programmes of both the government of the day and those of the other contenders for political office. What the youth think about elections and the electoral system is of importance to how they view their leaders and in motivating them to go to the polls.

Organs of civil society such as students' organisations, youth organisations, trade unions, churches and women's organisations have played leading roles in the various waves of the struggle for democracy. With the success of the democratisation process, they are now faced with the new challenge of participation in the new political dispensation. However, history shows that youth leagues have been misused by political party leaders to fulfil their own personal interests, rather than those of the nation, with the result that youth leagues became known as a destructive force in Lesotho. For example, in 1986 Major General Justin Lekhanya launched a military coup, during which Prime Minister Leabua Jonathan was arrested and a military executive, led by the Military Council, was instituted to rule Lesotho. The new military rulers claimed to have launched the coup in order to return the country to democratic rule through a process of national reconciliation. The Council rapidly granted amnesty to political prisoners and also disbanded the BNP Youth League, a move that was welcomed by the public since many had suffered at its hands. Vigilante youths had not only taken the law into their own hands, but also encouraged the proliferation of unauthorised weapons in the country. The disbanding of the BNP Youth League brought applause from a society weary of conflict.

Local government policy in Lesotho

Prospects and constraints

Good governance is heralded the world over as a pre-condition for sustainable development. Democratisation through decentralisation, among other things, is highly recommended as one of the strategies for, and indicators of, good governance. In an effort to promote democratisation for good governance, Lesotho formulated the Local Government Act 1997 as the legal instrument to guide decentralisation in the run up to, and into, the 21st century.

The present policy establishes local authorities to promote participatory governance and development throughout the rural and urban areas. In the rural areas, community councils and rural councils are established, while in the urban areas, urban councils and municipal councils are established as the local authorities.

Setting up community councils means establishing a regime, a culture and a new type of existence in the villages. People will need to forge new ways of interaction and create their own forms of reporting and service acquisition. It mirrors the birth of a new dispensation, almost the same way as gaining independence does. The challenge is now to deliver on this huge mandate by making the regime work.

In those community councils where, after the application of the provisions of Local Government Act of 1997 (as amended), the total number of councillors including two gazetted chiefs remains an even number, a coalition of opposition parties or independents is encouraged so as to grant them representation in the district councils. The aim is still to ensure that the district councils are as representative and inclusive as possible.

The magnitude of governance functions will determine which may be transferred to local government by the ministries. Some ministries have indicated which functions will be transferred as well as the officials who will be charged with delivering them on behalf of the ministries, in accordance with the principle of 'resources follow functions'.

Organisation and expertise already exists in the villages. Councils will then contribute by extending accountability so that officials know where to receive their remuneration and tools and also where to report their concerns and problems. Until the councils have stabilised, the districts will provide the usual assistance in the form of technical backstopping until the councils take full charge of their operations. Once the Local Government Service Commission is established, it will assume responsibilities for the recruitment of local government staff. The goal is to develop an attractive local government setup that will generate its own human, financial and material resources without depending on the central government, thus effectively harnessing the strengths of the people who created it through elections.

Notes

1   After the election, an election auditing initiative was set up by the governments of Botswana, South Africa and Zimbabwe to investigate possible election irregularities. This initiative was led by Judge Pius Langa. The release of the Langa Commission Report was mismanaged and its findings were greatly delayed. Although it stated that the election had administrative problems it concluded that no signs of rigging could be found. This led to an escalation in violent conflict because the report investigated the election but failed to realise that the electoral system and its exclusionary nature was in fact at the root of the conflict.

2   In 1998 Lesotho was plunged into chaos when 246 businesses were burnt down (incurring damages of up to R3 billion) and more than 3 000 workers lost their jobs.

Political integration in the SADC region

Harmonisation of legislative bodies through electoral system reforms

Khabele Matlosa

Introduction

Deepening political integration requires, inter alia, harmonisation of institutions, rules and procedures for democratic governance at both regional and continental levels. This requires an enormous amount of coordination of political processes (as well as their harmonisation and synergy) for the achievement of democratic governance, which, in some sense, demands pooling of sovereignty. It is against this backdrop that we can understand the political significance of such institutions as the Pan-African Parliament (PAP) in relation to the democracy project of the African Union (AU). The AU has committed itself to pursuing economic and political integration in Africa through institutions such as the PAP and through regional economic communities and their respective legislative bodies. Whereas the PAP is likely to ensure institutionalisation of political integration through legislative bodies of the 53 member states of the AU, other complimentary initiatives in this direction include the governance project of the New Partnership for Africa's Development (NEPAD) which, among others, includes the African Peer Review Mechanism (APRM). Thus, all things being equal, the positive combined effect of the PAP, NEPAD and the APRM would be the deepening of political integration in the continent and progressive consolidation of the continent's democratic governance. However, the success of political integration at the continental level is highly dependent upon progress made at the sub-regional level through regional economic communities in all the five regions of the continent.

The 14 states that belong to Southern Africa have established the Southern African Development Community (SADC). Based upon the 1992 SADC Treaty adopted in Windhoek, Namibia, member states have committed themselves to pursuing economic and political integration in tandem. This is a new development since previously much emphasis was placed upon economic integration almost to the exclusion of political integration, with dire consequences for the region, for not only does economic integration remain a mirage, but political integration has also just begun.

Political integration in the SADC region is evolving through various initiatives and institutional structures. Among these is the SADC Parliamentary Forum (SADC-PF) which brings together various legislative bodies in the region with a view to harmonising parliamentary traditions. Thus, although national parliaments are represented in the PAP, it is important to note that regional institutions such as the SADC-PF, and/or the envisaged SADC Parliament, would play a key role in linking national legislative bodies and the PAP in the near future.

Over and above harmonising parliamentary traditions and cultures to achieve continental political integration through the PAP, regional states need to discover possibilities of harmonising their electoral processes, in particular the nature of the electoral system.

This article grapples with the challenges of regional cooperation, particularly the imperatives for political integration. We explore progress made thus far in regional cooperation through legislative bodies. We also review the significance of electoral systems for democratic governance with a view to demonstrating the centrality of these systems for the formation (and possibly, the effectiveness) of parliaments. The main workings of existing electoral models in the SADC region are explored and it is argued that there is a dire need for SADC member states to regularly review their electoral models not only with a view to adopting appropriate reforms, but also with a view to harmonising their institutional frameworks for the purposes of the larger political integration project.

Challenges for regional cooperation

A survey of the regional cooperation literature suggests that Africa in general, and Southern Africa in particular, have achieved modest cooperation mainly in the area of political solidarity and relative political unity through, for instance, the Organisation of African Unity (OAU), predecessor to the AU, and the Frontline States/ SADC, although little has been achieved in the area of economic integration in the face of accelerated globalisation (Mkandawire, 1998; Evans, Holmes and Mandaza, 1999; SAPES/UNDP/SADC, 2000; Sako and Ogiogio, 2002). The political significance of the regional cooperation efforts cannot be overemphasised even if economic benefits have been dismal. However, despite the impressive political gesture of solidarity and unity, political integration predicated upon a solid Pan-Africanist ideology has not yet been achieved. Pan-Africanism of the 1960s and 1970s is currently being rekindled in the form of President Thabo Mbeki's African Renaissance (Makgoba, 1999; Mandaza and Nabudere, 2002), which is an ideal that Africa's awakening, emancipation, sustainable development and prosperity can be achieved only through the unity of its people and nations. Prah notes that Pan-Africanism/African Renaissance is a democratic and emancipatory movement which "shares a common inspiration with the rest of humanity in its historical drive towards freedom, justice and self-determination. This ideal was never intended to be a xenophobic or inward-looking principle" (1999:57–58). At the ideological level, Pan-Africanism or its new variant, African Renaissance, ought to form a firm political foundation for sustainable regional cooperation in Africa in general and Southern Africa in particular. For a successful regional cooperation effort in the continent as a whole and Southern Africa in particular, political integration must, of necessity, precede economic integration or, at the very least, the two processes must proceed in tandem.

Various regions in Africa have experimented with regional cooperation schemes since the 1970s, most of which either collapsed, such as the East African Community, or delivered insignificant economic results, such as the Economic Community of West African States. However, Southern Africa still stands out as having a relatively impressive record of regional cooperation. This region has the longest enduring and relatively 'successful' customs union scheme in the form of the Southern African Customs Union (SACU), which dates as far back as 1910. Linked to the SACU is a monetary union among South Africa, Lesotho, Swaziland and Namibia in the form of the Common Monetary Area (CMA), which is traceable to the mid-1970s. The region also experimented with an economic coordination scheme in the form of the Southern African Development Coordination Conference (SADCC) between 1980 and 1992 with modest economic and political achievements (SAPES/UNDP/SADC, 1998; SAPES/UNDP/SADC, 2000). With political liberation in both Namibia (1990) and South Africa (1994), the regional states have steered regional cooperation towards deep integration of a developmental type giving pride of place to achievement of economic community and political integration in tandem.

This new wave of regional cooperation tries to build on the limited successes of SACU/CMA and modest achievements of the SADCC experiment up to the early 1990s. In like manner, attempts at a regional political community through the SADC Organ for Politics, Defence and Security aim at building upon the foundations of the now defunct Frontline States and strives towards collective security within the framework of the 1992 SADC Treaty. Southern African states aptly recognise that economic integration must proceed in tandem with political integration. As Chipeta reminds us, "the case of regional cooperation and integration must thus consider both economic and political motivations" (1999:34).

It is important from the onset to define and problematise a number of intertwined, albeit distinct, concepts that will recur in this paper as we proceed. These are (a) regional cooperation; (b) economic integration; (c) political integration; and (d) deep integration. Regional cooperation is a wide and open-ended concept referring to a variety of situations wherein individual states and peoples in a specific and well-defined region deliberately interact through formal and informal schemes and networks across boundaries for mutual gain. Such interactions are theoretically driven by imperatives of economic reciprocity (mutual economic gain) among states, pooling of sovereignty by giving allegiance to and abiding by rules set out by a supranational institution (mutual political gain) and daily survival of the ordinary peoples of a region. Regional integration can also be perceived as "an attempt by nation states to control at the regional level what they have increasingly failed to manage at the national and multilateral levels...[It] is a...form of international regulation designed to accommodate the contradictory requirements of flexibility; that is, to preserve and in some cases intensify the mobility of factors of production whilst at the same time limiting the threat of foreign competition" (Gibb, 1997:71). At the state level, regional cooperation includes situations in which countries share or make available to each other resources, technology and expertise, collaborate in joint projects or act together in external economic and other relations (Davies,

1994:12). At the non-state level, two major forms of regional cooperation are informal cross-border trade and migration (Matlosa, 2001a).

In a plethora of literature on regional cooperation, two important anomalies are noticeable: (a) conventionally, regional cooperation is linked merely to state-to-state interactions; and (b) regional cooperation is taken to be synonymous with economic integration. The first misconception suggests that much of the literature on regional cooperation is state-centric and disregards informal cross-border socio-economic interactions among ordinary peoples in their struggle for daily survival, irrespective of colonial boundaries which define state sovereignty. These informal interactions, which could also be seen as regional cooperation from below that clearly expresses popular sovereignty, challenge the legacy of settler colonialism and indiscriminate colonial boundaries. It is thus crucial that state-driven regional cooperation and people-driven regional cooperation are sufficiently harmonised. Recently Mandaza, Tostensen and Maphanyane noted correctly that regional cooperation and integration must have a popular region-wide constituency and this suggests, in and of itself, the need for democratisation of regionalism with a view to broadening participation of popular forces and addressing the immediate and long-term interests and needs of the region's peoples. Their conclusion is quite instructive: "after all it is the people, not the governments, who will integrate the economies and societies of Southern Africa. The challenge, therefore, is to release the inner dynamic of integration, to let the people i.e. the business communities, the artists, the sports people, the professionals and civil society as a whole to be the motor of the process" (1994:102).

The second misconception portrays regional cooperation as purely an economic process and specifically links cooperation primarily to inter-state trade. In this respect, much of the debate on regional cooperation will inevitably revolve around issues of trade creation and trade diversion, through the nexus of the Ricardian theory of comparative advantage. According to Evans, Holmes and Mandaza, "trade creation is simply new trade that would not otherwise occur, while trade diversion refers to trade taking place inside the region at the expense of the rest of the world...Trade creation occurs when reduction of trade barriers leads countries to import from their partners products which they were previously producing themselves...Trade diversion occurs when countries buy from their regional partners, as a result of preferential agreement, goods which they previously imported from the rest of the world" (1999:5-7).

To highlight the stark distinction between regional cooperation and economic integration it is worthwhile to conceive of regional cooperation as a broad term, encompassing within it three main forms. First, economic coordination denotes the lowest form of regional cooperation wherein policies, strategies and regulations of a specific group of states in a given region are harmonised to bring them into line with those of other cooperating states for mutual gain (Davies, 1994:12). Economic coordination may not necessarily lead to economic integration. The SADCC is a glaring example of regional economic coordination in Southern Africa, which was never meant to bring about economic integration at all. Second, regional economic integration depicts the highest form of regional cooperation wherein economies of individual states in a given region are merged either in whole or in part into a distinct entity – a single regional economy or market (Davies, 1994:12). Whereas economic coordination does not require economic integration in order to succeed, the latter does require the former as its prerequisite to deepen and sustain regional cooperation.

Third, a regional political community refers to another form of regional cooperation wherein states located in a specific region perceiving a common external threat join hands in a limited membership supranational organisation to address their political, military and diplomatic interests with a view to strive towards a collective/common security (Plano and Olton, 1988). Southern Africa's experience with regional political community has been in the form of the Frontline States between the mid-1970s and the early 1990s and the current SADC Organ for Politics, Defence and Security. It is abundantly evident, therefore, that all the three main forms of regional cooperation have their mark on the political economy of Southern Africa.

The concept of deep integration is employed in this paper to denote the simultaneous strive by SADC states for far-reaching economic integration and political integration at the same time or, better still, prioritising the latter over the former. In terms of economic integration, this approach entails "the removal of external barriers, like tariffs, as well as internal barriers, such as monopolies and cartels, investment licensing and regulations. In contrast, shallow integration is concerned with removing only the external barriers" (SAPES/UNDP/SADC, 2000:18). In terms of political integration, this approach denotes harmonisation of political systems, institutions and structures among member states to deepen political solidarity and unity with a view to not only consolidate and nurture democracy but also to ensure constructive management of costly, violent intra- and inter-state conflicts. This in part also presupposes the ceding (or, better stated, pooling) of sovereignty through a supranational institution such as the SADC.

It is widely accepted that countries are fast embracing regional cooperation as an important development strategy, particularly today under conditions of globalisation. Generally, it is assumed that regional cooperation is a prudent development policy path particularly for developing countries for the following interconnected reasons:

1. Increasing the size of the home market and so improving efficiency and the incentive for investment, trade and aid;
2. Enhancing scale economies thereby promoting a more rational use of factors of production i.e. land, labour and capital;
3. Reducing duplication in administration and so economising scarce resources;
4. Increasing bargaining power vis-à-vis foreign firms and governments as well as various other international fora;
5. Increasing specialisation, complementarity and the comparative advantage of cooperating states;
6. Harmonising and merging socio-political structures, institutions and values for mutual developmental gains;
7. Pooling of sovereignty through supranational institutions to achieve political integration for regional stability, peace and collective security; and
8. Institutionalisation of constructive conflict management in dealing with both intra-state and inter-state conflicts (see Gibb, 1997).

Regional cooperation through the legislative bodies

While Southern African states continue to pursue economic integration with vigour through the SADC, much still needs to be done to ensure that both economic and political benefits for integration are achieved. One of the major challenges facing the region is precisely how best to ensure political integration through key democratic institutions such as parliaments. Undoubtedly, the legislature plays an important role in any working and vibrant democracy. Although the legislature performs various functions, the main ones include:

1. Representation of the electorate;
2. Law making and policy approval;
3. Oversight and checks and balances;
4. Accountability; and
5. National budgeting and financial management.

The SADC experience suggests that parliaments do perform these roles, but the degree to which they actually succeed in achieving the intended objectives of these functions differs from country to country. However, the trend that seems to mark the general performance of parliaments is simply that the executive arm of government tends to stamp its political hegemony or dominance over the legislature such that the latter is constrained in terms of achieving the above objectives and in particular, the oversight role of parliament gets compromised. The dominance of the executive over the legislature in the SADC is further reinforced by the dominant party syndrome and the fragmented and enfeebled opposition parties both within and outside parliament. By all indications, Swaziland is one country in which the overbearing dominance of the executive, and indeed, the country's royalty, asphyxiate the democratic functioning of parliament as witnessed by the recent events that led to the dismissal of the Speaker of Parliament by the King on grounds of not toeing the line desired by the monarch. However, some parliaments, such as South Africa's, have managed to establish themselves as critical watchdogs over the executive even in the context of a dominant party system and this is one of the key challenges facing parliaments in the region and on the African continent. Be that as it may, the challenges confronting parliaments for the deepening of democratic governance are not confined to the domestic/national scene alone. The challenges extend beyond the national political landscape to encompass the imperatives for regional and continental political integration, as it were.

We are aware that the AU has made clear its intentions to steer the continent more and more towards regional integration at various planes, including political integration. It is in this context that the PAP was inaugurated in Addis Ababa, Ethiopia, in March 2004. The AU evolved as a successor to the OAU and was formally launched in 2002 in Durban, South Africa. The main organs of the AU include:
1. The Assembly;
2. The Executive Council;
3. The Commission;
4. The Permanent Representatives' Committee
5. The Peace and Security Council;
6. The PAP;
7. The Economic, Social and Cultural Council; and
8. The Court of Justice.

Thus, one of the key organs of the AU is the PAP. The aim of the PAP is to "evolve into an institution with full legislative powers, whose members are elected by universal adult suffrage". At present, the PAP is simply an advisory and consultative body with little legislative or oversight functions vis-à-vis the AU. Each member of the AU (53 states) is represented in the PAP by five MPs, representing the diversity of political opinions and gender mix in each national parliament. The main objectives of PAP are to:
1. Facilitate the effective implementation of the policies and objectives of the AU;

2. Promote the principles of human rights and democracy in Africa;

3. Encourage good governance, transparency and accountability of member states;

4. Familiarise the people of Africa with the objectives and policies aimed at integrating the African continent within the framework of the AU's establishment;

5. Promote peace, security and stability;

6. Contribute to a more prosperous future for the people of Africa, promoting collective self-reliance and economic recovery;

7. Facilitate cooperation and development in Africa;

8. Strengthen continental solidarity and build a sense of common destiny among the people of Africa; and

9. Facilitate cooperation among regional economic communities and their parliamentary fora.

Whereas national parliaments will play an important role in terms of ensuring the political integration of the African continent through the PAP, it is worth noting that regional legislative bodies are also poised to be at the centre of this whole process and could act as a bridge between the PAP and national parliaments. It is in this context that the key role to be played by the SADC-PF, based in Windhoek, Namibia, ought to be understood. It is worth noting that the SADC treaty of 1992 commits the supranational body to pursue both economic and political integration in tandem. It is certainly in this context that we are able to appreciate the significance and strategic importance of the work being undertaken by the SADC-PF. This comprises 12 parliaments of the region, representing about 1 800 MPs, with a mission to bring about convergence of economic, political and social values in the SADC and help create the appropriate environment for deeper regional cooperation through popular participation. The member states in the SADC-PF are Angola, Botswana, Lesotho, Malawi, Mauritius, Mozambique, Namibia, South Africa, Swaziland, Tanzania, Zambia and Zimbabwe. Its programmes include election observation, conflict management, gender equity in the legislatures, HIV/AIDS and governance, and inter-parliamentary cooperation and regional integration. The SADC-PF is doing marvellous work towards regional political integration in this part of the world through election observation, training MPs and developing norms and standards for elections. It is bound to become a critical factor linking national parliaments in the SADC region and the PAP at the continental level. It is worth noting, though, that at all levels (national, regional and continental) the effectiveness of parliaments in practicing democratic governance is inextricably linked to the way in which the legislature is constituted. This brings us closer to the issue of elections and electoral systems. The challenge for the SADC in this respect is that although regular elections have become a norm, regional states have not yet embraced the practice of review and reform (where appropriate) of their electoral systems. It is to this that the remainder of this chapter now turns.

Significance of an electoral system for democratic governance

An electoral system principally refers to an institutional arrangement for the conduct of an election, be it a local government, national assembly or presidential election. Put differently, an electoral system encompasses procedures, laws, rules and regulations for the electorate to exercise their democratic right to choose their leaders and translate those ballots into actual representation in the national assembly. According to Harris and Reilly, "An electoral system also has a major influence on the type of party system that develops: the number and relative size of political parties in parliament, and the internal cohesion and discipline of parties" (1998:191–192). This institutional arrangement in turn determines the manner in which votes cast by the electorate in an election are turned into seats in, for instance, the national assembly. According to Reynolds and Reilly, "electoral systems translate the votes cast in a general election into seats won by parties and candidates". As Harris and Reilly aptly put it, "In translating the votes in a general election into seats in the legislature, the choice of electoral system can effectively determine who is elected and which party gains power. Even with exactly the same number of votes for parties, one system might lead to a coalition government and another to a single party assuming majority control" (1998:191–2).

The key variables are the electoral formula used (i.e. whether the system is majoritarian or proportional and what mathematical formula is used to calculate the seat allocation) and the district magnitude (not how many voters live in a district, but how many members of parliament that district elects. Countries that use the first past the post (FPTP) electoral system include the United Kingdom, the United States of America, India, Canada and all former British colonies.

Andrew Reynolds reminds us that an electoral system is a critical institution that shapes and influences the rules of political competition for state power in that this single institution determines "what parties look like, who is represented in parliament, and ultimately who governs" (1999:89). Essentially, an electoral system performs many functions in a representative democracy. Harris and Reilly isolate three major functions of an electoral system. First, it acts as a conduit through which the electorate is able to hold their representatives in the legislature account-able. Second, it makes it easy for the national assembly to be constituted either through a proportionally determined vote count or through a simple plurality of votes. Third, different electoral systems bring out public opinion in the form of an electoral outcome by according a particular political party or a coalition of parties control of state power and as such, "give incentives to those competing for power to couch their appeals to the electorate in distinct ways. In deeply divided societies, for example, particular electoral systems can reward candidates and parties who act in co-operative, accommodative manner to rival groups; or they can instead reward those who appeal only to their own ethnic group" (Harris and Reilly, 1998:192).

To be sure, there are many electoral systems in the world and there is little con-sensus as to which is best for democratic governance and political stability (Harris and Reilly, 1998; Reynolds and Reilly, 2002; Kadima, 2003; Konrad-Adenauer-Stiftung, 2003). What is interesting to note, though, is that despite the centrality of an electoral system to the choice of a government, countries hardly ever make deliberate decisions to select a model that best suits their particular conditions and contexts. Thus, "often the choice is essentially accidental, the result of an unusual combination of circumstances, of a passing trend, or of a quirk of history, with the impact of colonialism and the effect of influential neighbours often especially strong" (Reynolds and Reilly, 2002:1). As Jackson and Jackson aptly observe, "each political system offers certain benefits and disadvantages in terms of the representation of different groups in society" (1997:371). Reynolds and Reilly advise appropriately that states should endeavour to review and deliberately design electoral systems that suit their own conditions with a view to deepening democratic governance. In doing so, they argue, it is advisable that eight key criteria are used to guide the process:
1. Ensuring a representative parliament;
2. Making elections accessible and meaningful;
3. Providing incentives for conciliation;
4. Facilitating stable and efficient government;
5. Holding the government and representatives accountable;
6. Encouraging "cross-cutting" political parties;
7. Promoting a parliamentary opposition; and
8. Cost and administrative capacity (2002:9–13).

Although there are, indeed, many electoral systems around the world and there is as yet no consensus within both academic and policy discourses on the best model for democracy, it is a lot easier to identify, on a global scale, the three main types of electoral systems. These are the plurality-majoritarian, proportional representation (PR) and semi-proportional representation systems, with multiple variations within and permutations among them. For an extensive discussion of how these systems operate, refer to Reynolds and Reilly (2002), Harris and Reilly (1998), Reilly (2001) and Elklit (2003), from which the current debate draws critical lessons for the SADC region. It is worth noting, though, that the major distinction between and among the electoral systems globally relates to how "they translate national votes won into parliamentary seats won: that is, how proportional they are" (Harris and Reilly, 1998:193). The key variable here is whether an electoral system determines parliamentary seats upon a simple plurality of votes, an absolute majority of votes or proportionality of votes, hence the differentiation between plurality-majoritarian systems and proportional representation systems. Before dealing with each category of electoral systems, highlighting their distinctive impact on democratic governance in respect of accountability, representation and political stability, a few caveats are worth making at this juncture.

First, there is no gainsaying that the most dominant influence for the adoption of particular electoral systems in post-independence SADC has been the overbearing colonial and neo-colonial linkages between the former colonies and the colonial metropolis. It should be recalled that SADC countries adopted the political institutions of their former colonial masters as part of the political settlement of the de-colonisation struggles. Let it be recalled also that a majority of the Southern African states were under British colonial rule and upon independence, they adopted the Westminster constitution and political arrangement that go with it. By the same token, it is worth refreshing our minds that very few Southern African states have thus far taken a deliberate effort to re-design their electoral systems in a manner that addresses the immediate challenges of their democratic systems, such as accountability, representation and political stability. Angola (1992) Mozambique (1994) South Africa (1994), Namibia (1990) and fairly recently Lesotho (2002) and Mauritius (2003) are the countries that have done so, while the rest of the SADC member states operate electoral systems that are part of the legacy of the political and constitutional arrangements inherited from the departing colonialists in the 1960s. It is thus no surprise that the British single-member plurality or the FPTP electoral system has become a dominant political feature of electoral democracy in the SADC region given Britain's dominant colonial role in the region.

Second, only recently have SADC states begun to engage in open public debate, mostly initiated by civil society organisations, to interrogate the utility of existing electoral systems in various countries for the nurturing and consolidation of democratic governance. This effort has let to the recent electoral reform process in

Lesotho, an historic process in which the ruling Lesotho Congress for Democracy (LCD) and the then-Interim Political Authority (IPA) agreed to change from the FPTP system to the mixed-member proportional (MMP) system, which was first put to the test in the country's 2002 general election. Likewise, Mauritius has also undertaken a review of its electoral system which is principally a FPTP system injected with a best-loser arrangement. Following a commission set up to review the electoral system and propose measures for electoral system reform, Mauritius was expected to adopt the MMP system in its 2005 election, which was highly recommended by the commission report. Whereas in Lesotho the pressures for electoral reform were propelled mainly by political instability and the tendency for the FPTP system to exclude critical political actors, in Mauritius the pressures had more to do with political exclusion rather than political instability as such.

Third, electoral engineering and reform measures in the SADC have also been part of the political settlement of protracted violent conflict. It should be recalled that Southern Africa was a theatre of violent and costly conflicts of various types, linked, in part, to the global Cold War of the time and propelled by apartheid destabilsation of the region. The countries that were hardest hit by the protracted violent conflict were Angola, Mozambique, Namibia and South Africa. It is no surprise, then, that upon political settlement of violent conflicts in these countries one of the imperatives for constructive management of the conflict was some reform of the electoral system, among many other steps taken by the belligerent parties. Thus, as part of the peace-making and reconciliation processes, all these four countries adopted the PR electoral system. With hindsight, its adoption by these war-torn countries was one of the most prudent decisions that the political leadership undertook for, in fact, it has come to pass that the PR system has helped these countries (bar Angola) to consolidate their hard-earned peace and build bridges between former enemies who are today sharing the burden of statecraft and nation-building. It can thus be argued convincingly that the PR electoral system is the best electoral model for war-torn societies and easily lends itself to constructive management of violent conflicts in such countries as the DRC, for instance.

Today a majority of SADC states (eight in all) operate the FPTP electoral system, four operate the List-PR electoral system and only two have adopted the MMP. All these systems have their own distinctive impact on democratic governance in each state in terms of accountability, representation and political stability. This is the subject of the next section of this chapter.

How electoral systems work and their implications for accountability, representation and political stability

The first past the post electoral system

The main features of the FPTP electoral system are presented below. Figure 1 does not bring out all the characteristics of the system, but highlights those that are important for our understanding of the workings of the system as well as its implications for and impact on accountability, representation and political stability.

Figure 1: Characteristics of the FPTP electoral system

Advantages	Disadvantages
Clear choice between two main parties	Excludes minor parties
Ensures single party governments	Exaggerates electoral dominance of ruling parties
Gives rise to coherent parliamentary opposition	Problem of wasted votes which amounts to disenfranchisement
Excludes extremist parties	Amenable to minority government problem
Links MP to constituency	Unresponsive to changes in public opinion
Allows independent candidates to contest elections	Open to manipulation of election boundaries
Allows floor crossing	Less conducive to women's participation
Simplicity and familiarity in Africa	Problem of single party parliament

The FPTP or single-member plurality system is the most widely used, and indeed the simplest, electoral system in the entire world. Under this system, a country is divided into different, albeit relatively equal, electoral zones known as constituencies from which contestants have to emerge in order to occupy their seats in the legislature. The winner of an election is the candidate "who gains the most votes, but not necessarily an absolute majority of the votes. Voters choose their favoured candidate with a tick or a cross on the ballot paper, and the winner is simply the candidate who gains a plurality of votes" (Reilly, 2001:15). Like all other electoral systems, the FPTP has its own strengths and weaknesses and it is important that political leaders and all other stakeholders in election management appreciate these in order to ensure a smooth process of electoral designs and reform efforts.

The popularity of the FPTP is premised primarily on "grounds of simplicity, and its tendency to produce representatives beholden to defined geographic areas"

(Harris and Reilly, 1998:194). Figure 1 above illustrates the main feature characteristics of the FPTP system, which in a sense succinctly suggests its strong and weak points that have to be recognized in any process of electoral engineering, design and reform. The key strengths of the FPTP system are many and varied. First, given that it basically ensures duopolistic party system (a two-party system, if you wish), it presents a clear choice for voters between the two main parties. Whereas this has been the case in the United States of America and the United Kingdom, for instance, in terms of alternate regime changes between the Democrats and Republicans and the Labour Party and Conservative Party respectively, this has not been the case in the SADC region. If anything, in all the SADC countries operating the FPTP, one-party dominance or hegemony has been the norm from independence to date, including in Botswana, the world-acclaimed liberal democracy (see Figures 3 and 4 below). That is why the major test of the profundity of Botswana's liberal democracy today is for that country to experience the electoral defeat of the ruling Botswana Democratic Party (BDP) and an opposition party taking over as a new government, with the socio-economic and political achievements of the country thus far not being reversed in any profound manner. This prospect will always remain a distant mirage so long as the FPTP still remains a feature of Botswana's political system. This point reinforces the downside of the FPTP system, which is that it exaggerates the electoral dominance of broad-based parties (often the ruling parties).

Figure 2: Botswana's parliamentary election results, 1999

Party	No. of votes	% of votes	No. of seats	% of seats
BDP	192 598	54.3	33	82.5
BNF	87 457	24.7	6	15.0
BCP	40 096	11.3	1	2.5
BAM	15 805	4.5	0	0.0
Independents	1 004	0.3	0	0.0
MELS	22	0.0	0	0.0
Spoilt ballots	17 481	4.9	–	–
Total	354 463	100.0	40	100.0

The picture of proportions of votes per party in Botswana since independence as shown in Figure 2 validates our argument that Botswana is, to all intents and purposes, a dominant party situation despite its receipt of accolades for being a shining liberal democracy. This situation is further depicted by the allocation of parliamentary seats since independence, as vividly illustrated in Figure 3 below.

Figure 3: Number of National Assembly seats by party in Botswana (1965–1999)

Party	1965	1969	1974	1979	1984	1989	1994	1999
BDP	28	24	27	29	29	31	27	33
BPP	3	3	2	1	1	0	0	0
BIP	0	1	1	0	0	0	0	0
BNF	–	3	2	2	4	3	13	6
BPU	–	–	–	–	0	0	0	0
BCP	–	–	–	–	–	–	–	1
BAM	–	–	–	–	–	–	–	0
Total	31	31	32	32	34	34	40	40

Source: Molomo, 2000; Somolekae, 2002

Second, and related to the first point, the FPTP system ensures single-party governments. It is not amenable to coalition governments. This feature is often considered to be good as it is perceived to ensure political stability. However, single party governments may amount to one-party states and lead to politics of exclusion that generate various types of conflicts and political instability, as the political history of the small mountain kingdom of Lesotho so vividly demonstrated up until the major violent conflict of 1998 which in turn led to the electoral reforms of 2002. The single-party phenomenon also links to the weakness of this system in that it encourages one-party parliaments, thereby undermining the watchdog role of the legislature vis-à-vis the executive organ of the state.

Third, the FPTP is also regarded as giving rise to a coherent parliamentary opposition. Again, this feature applies in circumstances where the opposition is able to win some constituency seats and form part of government. But in a majority of cases, the opposition is often unable to win enough seats to make it a viable force in the national assembly. Not only that, the FPTP system obviously leads to wasted votes – a phenomenon tantamount to disenfranchisement of a considerable segment of the electorate. Witness, for instance, the results of the general election in Lesotho in 1993 and 1998 in which the ruling party won so overwhelmingly that there was absolutely no possibility whatsoever for a parliamentary opposition. Given the skewed correlation between the outcome and representation in parliament, the outcome resulted in wasted votes as Figure 4 below clearly illustrates. In 1993, the BCP won all the 65 parliamentary seats with 75% of the votes cast but the other two parties (BNP and MFP), which received a combined total of 24% of valid votes cast, won no parliamentary seats. A similar trend repeated itself in the 1998 election when the LCD won 79 of the 80 seats with only 61% of the votes, while the BNP, BCP and MFP received no parliamentary seats yet garnered about 33% of the valid votes cast.

Figure 4: Lesotho's election results of 1993 and 1998

Year	Main parties	No. of votes	% of votes	No. of seats	% of seats
1993	BCP	398 255	74.7	65	100.0
	BNP	120 686	22.6	0	0
	MFP	7 650	1.4	0	0
	Total	532 978	100.0	65	100.0
1998	LCD	355 049	60.7	79	98.7
	BNP	143 073	24.5	1	1.3
	BCP	61 793	10.5	0	0
	MFP	7 460	1.3	0	0
	Total	582 740	100.0	80	100.0

This figure demonstrates the exclusionary tendency of the FPTP system, which in turn disallows official opposition in parliament and drives political conflict out of parliament into the streets. In this way it can generate violent conflicts, with dire consequences for democratic governance. In the contemporary political history of Southern Africa, only in Zimbabwe did the FPTP system allow the main opposition party – the Movement for Democratic Change (MDC) – a considerable representation in parliament since the 2000 election, almost tantamount to a two-party system, although the ruling party (the Zimbabwe African National Union-Patriotic Front – ZANU-PF) still exercises an enormous amount of political hegemony (see Figure 5 on the next page).

Figure 5: Zimbabwe parliamentary election results, 2000

Party/Representation	No. of votes	% of votes	No. of seats	% of seats
ZANU (PF)	1 205 844		62	51.7
MDC	1 171 167		57	47.5
Zanu-Ndonga	15 776		1	0.8
Other	114 186		0	0.0
Total	2 507 973	100.0	120	100.0

Source: Electoral Institute of Southern Africa

Of the total 120 elected parliamentary seats, the ruling ZANU-PF won a simple majority of 62 seats (about 49% of the total valid votes) while the main opposition, the MDC, secured 57 seats (about 46% of the total valid votes). ZANU-Ndonga came third with only one seat and less than 1% of the total valid votes.

Fourth, one of the virtues of the FPTP system is its ability to disallow extremist parties. While this feature is an important one in that it discourages fragmentation of the polity and the social fabric of already divided societies, it also leads to almost total alienation of minor parties. This is the area in which the FTPT suffers from the misrepresentation syndrome. In a word, it is a system that to all intents and purposes is the weakest on broad representation of key political forces in the management of public affairs of a nation and thus not suited at all for countries emerging from protracted violent conflict.

Fifth, the FPTP electoral system is also reputed for linking MPs directly to their constituencies. It is for this reason that it is, at least in theory, considered strong on accountability of MPs to the electorate for they contest elections as individuals representing their constituencies. This contrasts sharply with the PR system in which the party has more power over the MP and thus undermines accountability of the MP to the electorate. This point dovetails neatly into the sixth feature of the FPTP system, namely that it also allows independent candidates to contest elections in their own right. Finally, given that the FPTP is the most commonly used electoral model in the world it is the most familiar system to a majority of SADC countries and indeed the most simple of all the electoral systems.

Seventh, given that the winner of an election in any given constituency has to get a simple plurality higher than the other contestants rather than an absolute majority of votes, this leads to winners by minority votes both at the constituency level as well as at the national level – a phenomenon that often generates a legitimacy crisis for governments. Neither the candidates, nor parties that endorse candidates, need an absolute majority of votes to form a government. The most vivid demonstration of a minority government brought about by the FPTP system in contemporary times in the SADC region is surely the 2001 parliamentary election in Zambia, which the ruling Movement for Multiparty Democracy (MMD) won with a paltry 44%. Surely if a government wins an election with less than 50% of the total valid votes, this is simply a pyrrhic victory and such a government is bound to face serious problems of credibility in its policy initiatives and in the legitimacy of its very existence, both at home and abroad. Part of the legitimacy crisis of the current Zambian government under the leadership of Levy Mwanawasa is manifested by the ongoing court cases lodged by opposition parties questioning the electoral process and its outcome.

Proportional representation electoral systems

PR electoral systems are relatively more complex electoral models than the plurality-majority systems. While the plurality, especially the FPTP, electoral systems accord electoral victory to a party/candidate with a simple plurality of votes over other contestants, the PR systems essentially balance the party's share of national valid votes cast and the concomitant share of its legislative seats. In a word, each party's political track record in terms of national votes should be reflected in the composition of a parliament. For instance, if a dominant party wins around 60% of the total national vote, its share of legislative seats should also be around 60% and the same applies to a minor party winning around 20% of the national vote. It is thus the most inclusive and broadly representative of all electoral systems. Thus, Harris and Reilly conclude, "for many new democracies, particularly those that face deep divisions, the inclusion of all significant groups in the parliament can be an important condition for democratic consolidation. Outcomes based on consensus-building and power-sharing usually include a PR system" (1998:195). Countries that operate the PR electoral system include Denmark, Sweden, the Netherlands, Israel, Finland, Switzerland etc. Under the PR system, there are no geographic electoral zones as is the case in the FPTP electoral system, as the entire country forms one single constituency.

As with plurality-majority electoral systems, there are quite a number of variations of PR systems. This discussion will focus mainly on the List-PR and MMP varieties.

The List-PR system

Figure 6: Characteristics of the List-PR system

Advantages	Disadvantages
Fair translation of votes into legislative seats	Weak MP-constituency link and accountability
Inclusion of minority parties in the legislature	Gives too much power to the party
Inclusive and socially diverse list of candidates	Little room for independent candidates
Regional fiefdoms restricted	May provide a platform for extremist parties
Leads to power sharing and coalition governments	Instability of coalition parties
Less vote wastage	Less likelihood of dislodging a ruling party
Appropriate for post-conflict societies	Disallows floor-crossing
Conducive to gender-inclusive governance	Less known and less familiar in Africa

The List-PR electoral system is the variety of the PR system that is most widely used in various parts of the world, including Southern Africa. There are two main types of List-PR systems, namely the open or preferential list system and the closed or non-preferential list system. The former involves direct participation of the party rank-and-file in the determination of the party list for a general election. The latter gives much more power to the party in determining the list of party candidates for a general election. Given that the latter is the most common system in Southern Africa, we focus on this model. As Reynolds and Reilly remind us, "In its most simple form, List-PR involves each party presenting a list of candidates to the electorate, voters vote for a party, and parties receive seats in proportion to their overall share of the national vote. Winning candidates are taken from the list in order of their position on the list" (2002:61).

In the List-PR system, candidates do not contest elections as individuals in their own right, but as party candidates appearing on a predetermined party list. This explains why in the Southern African context the PR system does not provide room for independent candidates to contest elections, unlike the FPTP system. Voters also do not elect individuals but political parties. The party list of candidates is "usually equivalent to the number of seats to be filled" (Asmal and de Ville, 1994:6). As Jackson and Jackson observe, "essentially, ... in all party list systems the election is primarily to ensure that the legislature reflects the relative popularity of the parties: individual candidates are a secondary concern" (1997: 373).

Furthermore, MPs are accountable to the party rather than to voters. Hence, the PR is usually criticised for its inability to ensure the accountability of the MP to the electorate, while subjecting him/her to the dictates of the party leadership. The winner is determined by a calculation of the total proportion of votes for each party relative to the overall valid votes cast. Using a threshold for qualification of parties to enter parliament (e.g. 0.25% in South Africa or 5% in Mozambique), qualifying parties are allotted parliamentary seats in equal proportion to their electoral strengths. The system has many positive tenets as depicted in Figure 6.

First, the List-PR system allows a fair translation of votes into parliamentary seats in that all parties contesting elections are able to get a fair share of their parliamentary representation depending upon their electoral performance and the entry threshold. However, it must also be pointed out that criticism has been levelled against the system in that it allows even minority or extremist parties to be represented in parliament and that this introduces a spoiler factor that could destabilise the political system.

Second, unlike the FPTP system, the PR system is reputed to encourage more inclusive and broadly representative mechanisms of governance. Hence, it lends itself easily to coalition governments. Undoubtedly, coalition governments could be a recipe for political instability especially in young and fragile democracies. However, if they are well managed coalition governments, or what are also referred to as governments of national unity, this can prove useful in the process of peace building, reconciliation and nation building as the Mozambican and South African experiences clearly show. The inclusivity and broad representativity of the Mozambican electoral system can be demonstrated by the nature of the election outcomes in 1999 (see Figure 7).

Figure 7: Mozambique's election results, 1999

Party	No. of votes	% of votes	No. of seats	% of seats
Frelimo	2 005 703	48.5	133	53.2
Renamo	1 603 811	38.8	117	46.8
Other	532 789	12.7	...	0.0
Total	4 132 303	100.0	250	100.0

Source: Electoral Institute of Southern Africa

In this way, the PR system has been found to be extremely useful as a conflict resolution mechanism, especially for countries emerging from violent conflicts such as Mozambique, Namibia and South Africa (Harris and Reilly, 1998; Reilly, 2001; Reynolds and Reilly, 2002; Konrad-Adenauer-Stiftung, 2003).

There is abundant evidence suggesting, in fact, that a major contributor to the resolution of the protracted violent conflict in Namibia, for instance, was the adoption of the PR electoral model following a negotiated settlement of the conflict. Namibia, like South Africa and Mozambique, boasts a fairly inclusive and broadly representative national assembly due in large measure to the PR system, as Figure 8 below vividly illustrates. As a conflict resolution mechanism, this system could also serve countries like the DRC well to entrench peace and security at least as part of the political settlement of the war. This suggests that before the PR system could contribute positively to a constructive management of a conflict, a solid peace agreement to which all belligerent parties adhere must be in place (Kumar, 1998; Matlosa, 2001b).

Figure 8: Namibia's election results, 1999

Party	No. of votes	% of total votes	No. of seats	% of seats
COD	53 289	10	7	9.7
DCN	1 797	0	0	0.0
DTA	50 824	9	7	9.7
FCN	764	0	0	0.0
MAG	3 618	1	1	1.4
SWANU	1 885	0	0	0.0
SWAPO	408 174	76	55	76.4
UDF	15 685	3	2	2.8
Total	536 036	100.0	72	100.0

Key: COD: Congress of Democrats; DCN: Democratic Coalition of Namibia; DTA: Democratic Turnhalle Alliance; FCN: Federal Convention of Namibia; MAG: Monitor Action Group; SWANU: South West African National Union; SWAPO: South West Africa People's Organisation; UDF: United Democratic Front.

It is also no wonder that South Africa also adopted the PR electoral model since its political transition in 1994. Figure 9 below depicts how inclusive this model is and how it accommodates all key political forces in an otherwise divided society. We demonstrate how the system has been able to ensure broad representation of various actors in South Africa's evolving democracy between 1994 and 2004. Even though the ruling African National Congress (ANC) has, by all indications, won all three elections with huge margins, entrenching a dominant party system, the country's democracy is surely thriving and the country's parliament is reputed to play a critical role in holding the executive accountable to the electorate.

Figure 9: South African National Assembly results, 1994–2004

Party	1994			1999			2004		
	Votes	%	Seats	Votes	%	Seats	Votes	%	Seats
ACDP	88 104	0.45	2	228 975	1.43	6	250 272	1.60	6
AEB	…	…	…	46 292	0.29	1	…	…	…
ANC	12 237 655	62.65	252	10 601 330	66.35	266	10 878 251	69.68	279
AZAPO	…	…	…	27 257	0.17	1	41 776	0.27	2
DP/DA	338 426	1.73	7	1 527 337	9.56	38	1 931 201	12.37	50
FA	…	…	…	86 704	0.54	2	…	…	…
ID	…	…	…	…	…	…	269 765	1.73	7
IFP	2 058 294	10.54	43	1 371 477	8.58	34	1 088 664	6.97	28
MF	13 433	0.07	0	48 277	0.30	1	55 267	0.35	2
NNP	3 983 690	20.39	82	1 098 215	6.87	28	257 824	1.65	7
PAC	243 478	1.25	5	113 125	0.71	3	113 512	0.73	3
GPDP	…	…	…	9 193	0.06	0	0	0	0
SOPA	…	…	…	9 062	0.06	0	14 853	0.10	0
UCDP	…	…	…	125 280	0.78	3	117 792	0.75	3
UDM	…	…	…	546 790	3.42	14	355 717	2.28	9
FF/FF+	424 555	…	9	127 217	0.80	3	139 465	0.89	4
AITUP	…	…	…	10 611	0.07	0	…	…	…
	19 533 498	…	400	15 977 142	89.30	400	15 612 667	99.37	400

Source: Lodge, 1999; IEC Report, 1999, 2004.

Fourth, the PR system is considered more conducive to enhancing gender equality in politics and increased participation of women, while the FPTP system is the weakest on this front (Molokomme, 2000). In a recent study, Molokomme discovered that although PR by itself is not a sufficient guarantee of increased women's participation in the legislature and cabinet, it is surely a catalyst for gender equality in the political governance arena. Figure 10 depicts women's participation in parliament in the SADC region and from this figure evidently those countries using the PR electoral system are doing much better than those using the FPTP.

Figure 10: Women in parliament in the SADC region

Country	Election	Seats	Women	% Women	Electoral system
Angola	1992	224	34	15	PR
Botswana	1999	47	8	18	FPTP
DRC	1970	210	–	–	FPTP
Lesotho	2002	120	12	10	MMP
Malawi	1999	193	16	8	FPTP
Mauritius	1995	65	5	8	Block vote
Mozambique	1999	250	71	28	PR
Namibia	1999	72	19	19	PR
Seychelles	1998	33	8	24	Mixed
South Africa	2004	400	131	33	PR
Swaziland	1998	95	7	7	FPTP
Tanzania	1995	275	45	16	FPTP
Zambia	1996	150	16	10	FPTP
Zimbabwe	2000	150	13	9	FPTP

Source: Molokomme, 2000

SADC states signed the declaration on gender and development during the 1997 summit in Blantyre, Malawi. The summit committed member states to equal gender representation in all key organs responsible for decision-making by the state. In this regard, member states committed themselves to achieve at least 30% representation of women in decision-making structures by the year 2005. It is in this context that Figure 10 above must be understood. It is clear from this figure that the top four countries in terms of women's representation in parliament are South Africa (33%), Mozambique (28%), Seychelles (24%) and Namibia (19%). Three of these operate the PR system, while one operates a majoritarian (Block Vote) system. The bottom four countries in terms of women's representation are Swaziland (7%), Malawi (8%), Mauritius (8%) and Lesotho (10%). It is instructive that three of these operate the FPTP (plurality) system, while one operates an MMP system. A plausible argument can be made, therefore, that the PR system is surely better for the enhancement of gender equality in the legislature. The MMP is the next best system, while the FPTP is the worst-case scenario for increased women's participation in the legislature. Be that as it may, it should be borne in mind, though, that on its own an electoral system is not enough to ensure gender equality in politics; there is a need for commitment by politicians to ensure gender balance through deliberate strategies such as quotas and/or reserved seats and/or zebra lists, such as the one adopted by the ruling ANC in South Africa. Furthermore, it is abundantly evident that the PR system is more useful for constructive management of conflicts, especially for countries emerging from protracted violent wars such as the DRC. The FPTP system has been identified as one of the various factors behind different types of both violent and non-violent conflicts in countries such as Lesotho, Zambia and Zimbabwe, although it has not necessarily triggered conflicts of such magnitude in Botswana and Mauritius.

Mixed-member proportional electoral system

The most basic features of the MMP electoral system are summarised in Figure 11 below. Since its major elements are more or less similar to a combination of the PR and the FPTP systems, I have avoided a detailed discussion of these elements, which have already been discussed above.

Figure 11: Characteristics of the MMP system

Advantages	Disadvantages
Retains accountability of MPs inherent in FPTP	Relatively more complex than the FPTP and PR
Retains broad representation in the legislature inherent in PR	Lack of familiarity in Africa since it is relatively new on the continent
Widens the political complexion of parliament (inclusiveness)	May lead to a fragmented parliament
Combination of constituency vote and party-list vote	Double voting either in a two ballot or single ballot system
Establishment of entry threshold for MPs to hold seats in parliament	Calculation of an entry threshold into parliament by MPs rather lengthy negotiation and consensus among parties
Facilitates power-sharing in the legislature	Rather costly relative to the FPTP
Opens avenues for gender balance	May generate a proliferation of parties in the legislature

On the basis of the above figure, the most vivid features of the MMP are as follows:

1. A portion of the parliamentary seats are determined on the basis of constituency votes;
2. Another portion is determined on the basis of party votes;
3. The system allows for the use of a double ballot through either two votes on one single ballot or two votes on two separate ballot papers;
4. Independent candidates can only contest elections in the constituency-based voting; and
5. A threshold or quota is devised and used for both the determination of winners and composition of an elected parliament.

Thus, the MMP in general aims to broaden representation (through the PR component), retain accountability of elected representatives (through the FPTP component) and, given its inclusiveness, can add considerable value to political stability. A country like Lesotho, for instance, had operated the FPTP electoral model bequeathed from the British colonial rule since independence in 1966. The country's historical record points to a disturbing trend of violent and non-violent conflict, mostly election-related. It was thus with a political history of election-related turbulence in the small mountain kingdom that electoral reform was subjected to public debate and finally the FPTP system was jettisoned in favour of the MMP system in May 2002. Thus, Lesotho "became the first African country to test the MMP electoral model in a parliamentary election"(Elklit, 2002:1). Lesotho used this electoral model during the 2002 national assembly elections for the first time (see Elklit, 2002). Its main tenets are summed up in Figure 11.

Surely, given the positive result of the MMP electoral model following the May 2002 election in Lesotho, there is no doubt that much of the spotlight in the democracy discourse in the SADC region will focus on Lesotho as regional states attempt to review and reform their electoral models.

Although a case can strongly be made that some SADC states will do well to reform their electoral models along these lines, it is also important to note that those countries that have just emerged from violent protracted conflict (such as the DRC, among others) will certainly be better served by the PR systems, if the experiences of Mozambique, Namibia and South Africa are anything to go by (see Kadima, 2003). Elklit says "there can be no doubt that the experiences from this first national level application of this electoral system to African soil will be studied carefully in many quarters, including outside the mountain kingdom. This is because discussions about possible electoral system changes are now part of the political discourse in many African countries or have been so recently. Countries where the MMP model has already been discussed include South Africa (where MMP is applied in local government elections), Tanzania, Zimbabwe and Mauritius" (2002:1).

It should be noted, though, that compared with the FPTP electoral model, the MMP is rather complex. This is because it actually combines two systems into one composite hybrid. In fact, the most difficult aspect of this system has to do with a formula for entry of MPs into the legislature and allocation of parliamentary seats. The value of the new MMP electoral system to Lesotho's fledgling and fragile democratic governance is demonstrated by the extent to which this model has changed the complexion of the national assembly, as Figure 12 on the next page vividly demonstrates.

Figure 12: Election results in Lesotho: 1965, 1970 and 2002

Year	Main parties	No. of votes	% of votes	No. of seats	% of seats
1965	BNP	108 162	41.6	31	51.6
	BCP	103 050	39.7	25	41.7
	MFP	42 837	16.5	4	6.7
Total		259 825	100.0	60	100.0
1970	BCP	152 907	49.8	36	60.0
(annulled)	BNP	120 686	42.2	23	38.3
	MFP	7 650	7.3	1	1.7
Total		285 257	100.0	60	100.0
2002	LCD	304 316	54.8	77	65.3
	BNP	124 234	22.4	21	17.8
	BAC	16 095	2.9	3	2.5
	BCP	14 584	2.7	3	2.5
	LPC	32 046	5.8	5	4.2
	NIP	30 346	5.5	5	4.2
	LWP	7 788	1.4	1	0.8
	MFP	6 890	1.2	1	0.8
	PFD	6 330	1.1	1	0.8
	NPP	3 985	0.7	1	0.8
Total		554 386	100.0	118	100.0

Source: Matlosa, 2003

The MMP system has great potential to deepen democratic governance and ensure political stability in Lesotho. The electoral reform process should not be confined to the political elite alone. The process must involve all sectors and sections of society from the planning stages, through design stages up to the implementation and review stages. This is an area where the Lesotho reform process has been weakest and this required a vigorous voter education prior to the 2002 election. The reform process must also lead not just to an adoption of a particular MMP because it is implemented in New Zealand and Lesotho, but it must be in accord with the particular political culture of each one of the SADC states. In other words, the electoral reform process must be homegrown and driven by a national vision rather than being externally derived and driven by aid donors (Matlosa, 2003).

As in the Lesotho case, Mauritius has also embarked upon a deliberate process of electoral system reform. It is interesting to note that whereas the electoral system reform in Lesotho was informed and driven more by the desire to reverse an age-old pervasive phenomenon of political instability, in the case of Mauritius the main driving motive was to entrench an already mature and relatively stable multiparty democracy. In the entire SADC region, the two main relatively mature and stable liberal democracies are surely Botswana and Mauritius. Among many internationally acclaimed attributes of the Mauritian democracy is the holding of regular elections and hence installation of legitimate and credible governments. Mauritius has thus been renowned for its constitutionally entrenched democratic tradition of regular elections since its independence in 1968. It has operated fundamentally a British-style FPTP electoral system. In contrast to the Lesotho FPTP, the Mauritian FPTP was improved by the introduction of a compensatory mechanism known as the Best Loser System (BLS), which was an attempt to improve on the deficit of FPTP in relation to broader representation and inclusivity of the system and by extension, broader participation of parties in the national assembly. Despite the compensation factor introduced by the BLS, Mauritius has not been satisfied with the FPTP system in terms of value added to its democratic governance.

The most recent election held in Mauritius on the 11 September 2000 still demonstrates the inadequacies of the FPTP. The election outcome witnessed the Militant Socialist Movement and Mauritian Militant Movement (MSM-MMM) alliance claiming state power on a paltry 51.7% of the total valid votes and grabbing all of the 60 parliamentary seats. Although this disequilibrium is compensated for by the BLS, the negative effect of the FPTP system on Mauritius's flourishing democracy still remains. Thus, despite the BLS mechanism, the FPTP system still has a number of deficiencies which prompted the government in Mauritius to engage a commission specifically to introduce a PR component, bringing it close to the MMP system.

It is abundantly clear from the cases of Lesotho and Mauritius that there are commendable efforts underway in the SADC region towards electoral reforms and these efforts are certainly bound to nurture the region's democratic governance. Hopefully, various other SADC member states will follow these examples and revisit their electoral models with a view to deepening and consolidating their democratic governance too.

Electoral reform imperatives in the SADC region

If democratic consolidation is to take root and be firmly institutionalised in the SADC region, regional states have to review and re-design their electoral models to suit their own peculiar historical and social conditions. Very rarely have states in the region deliberately embarked upon electoral reforms. As Reynolds and Reilly aptly observe, "If it is rare that electoral systems are deliberately chosen, it is rarer still that they are carefully designed for particular historical and social conditions of a country" (Reynolds and Reilly, 2002:1). So far, only Namibia (1990), Angola (1991), Mozambique (1992) and South Africa (1994) reformed their electoral models following the political settlement of their protracted conflicts, although Angola reverted back to war when the opposition did not accept the result. These countries have adopted the PR electoral system as we have already pointed out. This development was the culmination of the negotiations that aimed to end violent conflict. Thus, it could be argued that the adoption of the PR system in some countries, such as Namibia, Mozambique and South Africa, was indeed part and parcel of a constructive management of a conflict. In a sense, therefore, an electoral model could then be perceived as a conflict resolution mechanism. From these three cases, we can argue strongly that the PR system is a perfect model for war-torn societies emerging from deep-seated violent conflicts. Furthermore, in the recent past, Lesotho (2002) and Mauritius (2003) have reformed their electoral models in order to deepen their democratic governance regimes. In the case of the former, the main catalyst for the reform exercise had to do more with concerns around political stability while in Mauritius's case, the main propellent of reform was imperatives for broadening political representation in the legislature.

Having said this, though, the Angolan case also suggests that the electoral model alone is not a sufficient ingredient for a constructive resolution of a violent conflict. Angola operates the PR electoral model and many observers thought it was making good progress in the early 1990s towards a resolution of its long drawn-out war, especially following the Bicesse Accords. This was not to be, as the 1992 election was aborted by UNITA's refusal to accept the election outcome. This situation, however, does not invalidate our thesis that the PR system is a perfect model for resolution of protracted violent conflict. What it does suggest, though, is that the PR system can play a conflict resolution role in these circumstances only if the belligerent parties sign a peace agreement and abide by the letter and spirit of the agreement. This was the case in Namibia, Mozambique and South Africa (see Lodge, 2003, for instance). This was not the case in Angola in respect of both the 1991 Bicesse Accords and the subsequent 1994 Lusaka Accord. In other words, the electoral engineering in Angola, unlike in the other three countries, lacked a critical anchor in the form of a meaningful and sustainable peace.

As argued earlier, a majority of SADC member states operate the FPTP electoral system. Of all these, Zimbabwe is the most fascinating in terms of the historicity of electoral engineering and how this country ended up with the FPTP. Post-independence Zimbabwe adopted a semi-PR electoral model during its 1980 elections, as part of the Lancaster House political compromise, but later changed this model and adopted the FPTP system. It is not quite clear why Zimbabwe changed its electoral model in the mid-1980s, but what is obvious is that this was a major retrogression for the political system of that country as it formed part of various triggers for political centralisation and then the hyper-presindentialism that has emerged since the mid-1980s. There have been calls from various political forces and civil society organisations in Zimbabwe for electoral reform since the early 1990s. In fact, one major issue upon which the diametrically opposed government-led Constitutional Commission and the civil society-led National Constitutional Assembly were agreed upon during the 2000 constitutional review exercise was the reform of the Zimbabwe electoral model away from the FPTP towards some form of semi-PR model. In any case, electoral reform was already proposed in the draft constitution by the Constitutional Commission, which was rejected during the 2000 national referendum. This issue has to be revisited as a matter of urgency as part of a long-lasting solution to Zimbabwe's current political crisis.

Of the SADC countries operating the FPTP system with impeccable results both for economic progress and political stability, Botswana and Mauritius stand out. Botswana has operated the FPTP system since its political independence and, unlike in Swaziland and Lesotho, has never experienced any major form of political turbulence. That explains, in part, why Botswana is rightly considered a relatively mature and institutionalised liberal democracy in the SADC region. Although Botswana has not experienced political instability as a result of the FPTP electoral model as such, it still has to review and re-design this model. Such a review and electoral reform will help address the problem of lack of broad representation and the need for greater participation by other political forces in the political system, partly by down-scaling the political hegemony of the ruling BDP. It is imperative that as Botswana undertakes its electoral reform, it learns lessons from the experience of both Lesotho and Mauritius.

Both the Zambian and the Tanzanian situations also point to a dire need for electoral reforms, especially following their conflict-ridden general elections of 2001. The violent conflict that marked the general election in Tanzania, especially in Zanzibar, is clear evidence of the deficiencies of the FPTP system. Violent conflict also marked the Zambian election of the same year. A causal linkage between violent conflict and the FPTP in both Zambia and Tanzania may appear tenuous at first glance. Actually, the causal link is real in that losing parties know that even if they were to make considerable inroads in galvanising votes, they would neither capture state power nor be represented in the legislature given the degree to which the FPTP system exaggerates the electoral dominance of ruling parties. A similar spate of violent conflicts rocked Lesotho's political system from the 1970s until when the electoral model was changed from the FPTP to the MMP, as illustrated vividly earlier on. It is imperative, therefore, that Tanzania and Zambia consider seriously reforms to their electoral models before their next general elections in 2006. Lessons learnt from Lesotho and Mauritius clearly makes the MMP a suitable electoral model for Tanzania and Zambia.

Both the DRC and Swaziland are rather eccentric cases in comparison with the other SADC countries under review in this paper. Unlike other countries, the major challenge for democratic governance is really not so much the electoral reform per se. In Swaziland, the major challenge of governance revolves around the reform of the entire political system away from dynastic oligarchy towards multi-party democratic governance. Having settled this bigger challenge, Swaziland then has to consider electoral reform. Thus, the Swaziland case suggests that a country cannot consider reforming an electoral system until and unless the institutional, systemic and cultural aspects of a working democracy are firmly in place. Swaziland should thus reform its political system towards a constitutional monarchy along the lines of Lesotho and then institutionalise multipartyism in which the King remains the head of state and the prime minister becomes an effective head of government. Having done this, Swaziland should then proceed to adopt the MMP system along the lines followed in either Lesotho or Mauritius. The major challenge of governance in the Democratic Republic of Congo (DRC) revolves mainly around the consolidation of the country's fragile peace and commitment of all the belligerent parties to peace building, reconciliation and nation building. On the basis of this, a political climate must exist for the holding of elections. However, even before the election is held inter-party consultations and national debate must lead to the choice of the appropriate electoral model. Given the profundity of the violent conflict in the DRC over the years, it is imperative that that country adopts the PR electoral model if it is to manage its protracted violent conflict more constructively. According to Harris and Reilly, "the most important electoral requirement for democratic transition is usually a system that maximizes inclusiveness, is clearly fair to all parties, and presents minimal areas for potential pre-election conflicts...These goals are best achieved by some form of regional or national list PR which ideally leads to a 'grand' or 'oversized' coalition government" (1998:201).

Conclusion

The African continent is surely making commendable progress towards institutionalisation of democratic governance. The AU is pursuing both economic and political integration in tandem. In order to achieve its objectives of political integration and advance the continent's democracy project, the AU has established the PAP, among several of its organs. This is indeed a commendable effort for it heralds political commitment by the continent's leaders to nurture and consolidate democratic governance, which has begun to take root in a majority of the AU's 53 member states. All things being equal, the positive impact of the combined effect of the PAP and the NEPAD governance initiative is likely to translate into deeper political integration at the continental level. However, this long-term goal is dependent upon the extent to which both economic and political integration succeeds at the sub-regional level. That is why, in Southern Africa for instance, the role of the SADC in achieving economic and political integration in tandem is so crucial not only for the regional cooperation project, but even for the AU's vision of continental integration at various levels.

Although there are various facets of political integration, this chapter has focused discussion upon integration through legislative bodies. Much as national parliaments have direct representation on the PAP, it is incontrovertible that regional legislative bodies such as the SADC-PF play a pioneering role in the regional and continental agenda of political integration. For political integration to succeed at both regional and continental levels, there is need for harmonisation of appropriate institutions, traditions, rules and procedures. It is in this context that African legislative bodies have to harmonise their diverse and variegated traditions and cultures across the continent. It is also imperative that African states make deliberate efforts to review and possibly reform their electoral systems with the aim of deepening political integration. We have identified the three widely used electoral systems in Southern Africa as the FPTP, the PR and the MMP. Whereas no single electoral system is the best and most perfect for nurturing and consolidating democratic governance, it is imperative that SADC states make deliberate efforts to design and review their electoral models taking into account the challenges of accountability, representation and political stability, among others.

References

Asmal, K. and De Ville, J. 1994. "An electoral system for South Africa", in Stegtler et al (eds.) Free and fair elections, Cape Town: Juta and Co. Ltd.

Chipeta, C. 1999. "Prospects for further economic integration in the SADC", SAPEM, 13 (2), November.

Davies, R. 1994. "Approaches to regional integration in the Southern African context", Africa Insight, 24 (1).

Elklit, J. 2002. "Lesotho 2002: Africa's first MMP elections", Journal of African Elections, 1 (2).

Elklit, J. 2003. "What electoral systems are available? An international perspective on the current debate in South Africa", in Konrad-Adenauer Stiftung, Electoral models for South Africa: Reflections and options, Seminar Report, Johannesburg, South Africa.

Evans, D., Holmes, P. and Mandaza, I. 1999. SADC: The cost of non-integration, Harare: SAPES Books.

Gibb, R. 1997. "Regional integration in post-apartheid Southern Africa: The case of renegotiating the Southern African Customs Union", Journal of Southern African Studies, 23 (1), March.

Harris, P. and Reilly, B. (eds). 1998. Democracy in deep-rooted conflict: Options for negotiators, IDEA Handbook Series: Stockholm, Sweden.

Jackson, R. and Jackson, D. 1997. A comparative introduction to political science, N. J: Prentice Hall.

Kadima, D. 2003. "Choosing an electoral system: Alternatives for the post-war Democratic Republic of Congo", Journal of African Elections, 2 (1).

Konrad-Adenauer-Stiftung, 2003. Electoral models for South Africa: Reflections and options, Seminar Report, Johannesburg, South Africa.

Kumar, K. (ed). 1998. Post-conflict, elections and democratization and international assistance, Boulder: Lynne Reinner Publishers.

Lodge, T. 2003. "How the South African electoral system was negotiated", Journal of African Elections, 2 (1).

Luckham, R., Goetz, A. and Kaldor, M. 2003. Democratic institutions and democratic politics, University of Sussex (mimeo).

Makgoba, W. 1999. <u>African Renaissance</u>, Tafelberg: Mafube Publishers.

Mandaza, I., Tostensen, A. and Maphanyane, M. 1994. <u>Southern Africa in search of a common future: From the conference to a community</u>, Gaborone: SADC Secretariat.

Mandaza, I. and Nabudere, D. (eds). <u>Pan-Africanism and integration in Africa</u>, Harare: SAPES Books.

Matlosa, K. 2001a. "Ballots or bullets: Elections and conflict management in Southern Africa", <u>Journal of African Elections</u>, I (I).

Matlosa, K. (ed). 2001b. <u>Migration and development in Southern Africa: Policy reflections</u>, Harare: SAPES Books.

Matlosa, K. 2003. "The electoral process and democratic governance in Lesotho: Lessons for the Democratic Republic of the Congo", <u>Journal of African Elections</u>, 2 (1).

Mkandawire, T. 1998. "Globalisation and Africa's unfinished agenda", in SAPES/ UNDP/SADC, Harare: SAPES Books.

Molokomme, A. 2000. Building inclusiveness in SADC's democratic systems: The case of women's representation in leadership positions, paper presented at the Southern African Elections Forum, Windhoek, Namibia, 11–14 June.

Molomo, M. 2000. "In search of an alternative electoral system in Botswana", <u>Pula</u>, 14 (1).

Plano, J. C. and Olton, R. 1988. <u>The International Relations Dictionary</u>, Santa Barbara: ABC-CLIO.

Prah, K. 1999. "African renaissance or warlordism", in Makgoba, W. 1999. <u>African Renaissance</u>, Tafelberg: Mafube Publishers.

Reilly, B. 2001. <u>Democracy in divided societies: Electoral engineering for conflict management</u>, New York: Cambridge University Press.

Reynolds, A. 1999. <u>Electoral systems and democratization in Southern Africa</u>, Oxford: Oxford University Press.

Reynolds, A. and Reilly, B. 2002. <u>International IDEA handbook of electoral system design</u>, Stockholm, Sweden.

Sako, S. and Ogiogio, G. 2002. Africa: Major development challenges and their capacity building dimensions, ACBF Occasional Paper No. 1.

SAPES/UNDP/SADC. 1998. Governance and human development in Southern Africa, Harare: SAPES Books.

SAPES/UNDP/SADC. 2000. Challenges and opportunities for regional integration in Southern Africa, Harare: SAPES Books.

Somolekae, G. 2002. "Botswana", in Lodge, T., Kadima, D. and Pottie, D. (eds) Compendium of elections in Southern Africa, Johannesburg: Electoral Institute of Southern Africa.

www.ingramcontent.com/pod-product-compliance
Lightning Source LLC
Chambersburg PA
CBHW080427270326
41929CB00018B/3188